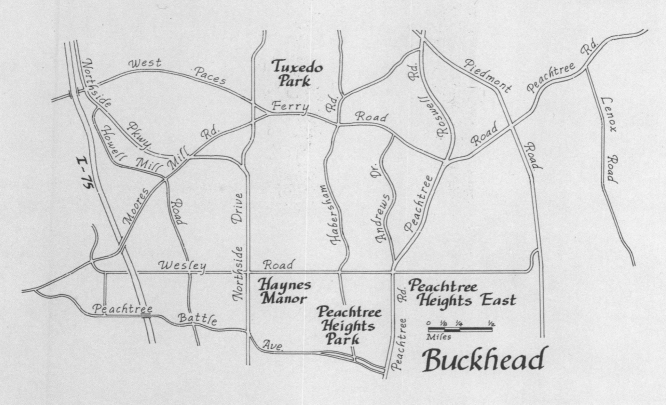

Buckhead

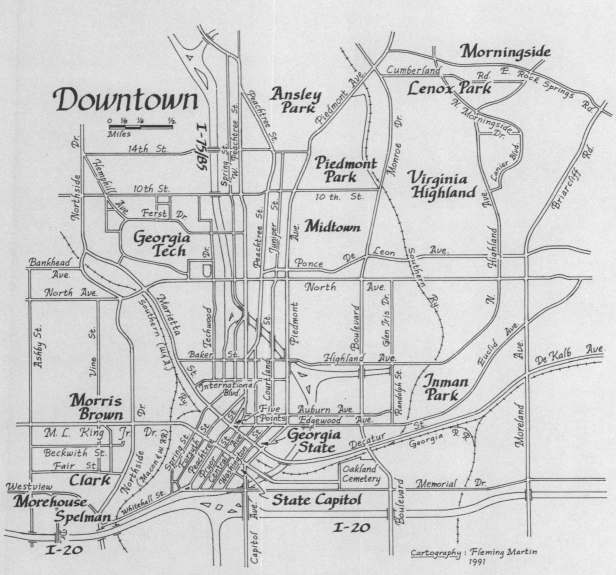

Downtown

Cartography: Fleming Martin
1991

CLASSIC ATLANTA

LANDMARKS OF THE ATLANTA SPIRIT

CLASSIC ATLANTA

LANDMARKS
OF THE ATLANTA SPIRIT

 WILLIAM R. MITCHELL, JR.

VAN JONES MARTIN

MARTIN~St. MARTIN
PUBLISHING COMPANY
NEW ORLEANS ❖ SAVANNAH

A GOLDEN COAST BOOK

CLASSIC ATLANTA *and other books published by Golden Coast and Martin-St. Martin are distributed by Peachtree Publishers, Ltd., 494 Armour Circle, NE, Atlanta, GA 30324; 800/241-0113*

Designed and produced by Van Jones Martin, Golden Coast Publishing Company, Savannah, Georgia.
Design assistance and supervision by Lisa Lytton-Smith, Charlottesville, Virginia.
Edited by Van Jones Martin, Rusty Smith, and William Mitchell.
Type set by Golden Coast and Savannah Color Separations.
Printed in Hong Kong by Everbest Printing Company, Ltd., through Four Colour Imports, Ltd., Louisville, Kentucky.

All photography © Van Jones Martin except as noted.

Credit for illustrations.
Dust jacket and pages 1–15, all photographs by Van Jones Martin except as follows: Atlanta Historical Society: ix; xi; 13; 14.
Timeline and gazetteer, pages 16–63, all photographs from the collection of the Atlanta Historical Society, except as follows: Collection of William R. Mitchell, Jr.; 16; James R. Lockhart: 31.2; 34.2; 41.3; 42.5; 43.1; 43.2; 44.2; 45.1; 45.2; 46.2; 47.1; Van Jones Martin: 31.1; 32.1; 32.2; 37.2; 37.3; 41.1; 46.1; 50; 53 center, bottom left, and bottom right; 58 lower and bottom; 59 bottom; 60 lower and bottom; 62 center; 63 top; Bill Hull: 37.1; 44.1; Michael Siede: 48.1; Cousins Properties: 49.1; William R. Mitchell, Jr.: 32.3; 35.4; 59 top; 63 center; John Portman and Associates: 48.2 (Lowell Williams, photographer); Heery International: 48.3.
All photographs on pages 64–223 are by Van Jones Martin with the following exceptions: James R. Lockhart: 94; 109 top. Atlanta Historical Society: 219.
Map on endsheets by Fleming Martin.

Frontispiece: Dorsey-Fraser house. Hentz, Reid & Adler, 1925.
Garden façade, Habersham Road.

Library of Congress Catalog Card Number: 91-71487
ISBN 0-932958-12-5

To
the enduring and indomitable
Atlanta Spirit
and the preservation
of its landmarks.

TABLE OF CONTENTS

ACKNOWLEDGMENTS   *viii*

ATLANTA HISTORICAL SOCIETY COLLECTIONS   *ix*

PREFACE   *x*

INTRODUCTION: *The Atlanta Spirit*   *12*

The Atlanta Spirit in Architecture: A Timeline   *16*

Landmarks of Atlanta Residential Architecture   *50*

Landmark Homes of Atlanta   *64*

EPILOGUE   *218*

BIBLIOGRAPHY   *220*

A CENTURY OF ARCHITECTS   *222*

INDEX OF HOUSES   *223*

Opposite: Memorial and ginkgo trees at entrance to Peachtree Heights Park.

ACKNOWLEDGMENTS

PREPARING THE MANUSCRIPT—researching and writing—and seeing to illustrations, including photographs, old and new, required over two years, during which Van and I asked numerous people for help. I want first to acknowledge homeowners and house supervisors, whom I interviewed: Mr. W. Wesley Adams; Mr. Robert B. Aiken; Mrs. Dameron Black III; Mrs. Bates Block; Mr. Joseph W. Blount; Callanwolde Fine Arts Center staff; Mr. and Mrs. Thomas Hal Clarke; Mrs. Julian S. Carr; Mrs. Beverly M. Du-Bose, Jr.; Mr. and Mrs. J. Ray Efird; Mr. Daniel B. Franklin; Mrs. Dejongh Franklin; Mr. Luis Garcia; Governor's Mansion, Mrs. Joe Frank Harris and staff; Mr. Robert N. Griggs; Mr. and Mrs. William Griffin; Mrs. Bradley Hale; Herndon Home, staff; Mr. and Mrs. W. Barrett Howell; Mrs. Edward H. Inman; Mr. Comer Jennings; Mrs. Frank C. Jones; Dr. George W. Jones, Jr.; George Lanier, Esq.; Mr. and Mrs. Edward McCord, Shellmont Lodge; Mrs. Michael A. McDowell; Mrs. Thomas E. Martin, Jr.; Mr. Joseph Mayson; Mrs. Howard J. Morrison, Jr.; Drs. Dale and Barbara Ray; Reynolds Cottage, Spelman College, Dr. Johnnetta B. Cole, Jo Moore Stewart, Pat Anderson, and staff; Rhodes Hall, Tommy Jones and other members of the Georgia Trust for Historic Preservation staff; Mr. and Mrs. William A. Rooker, Jr.; Mrs. Henry B. Tompkins; Mr. and Mrs. Wayne M. Watson; Carol Mumford and Karen Kelley at the Wren's Nest.

Oakland Cemetery.

Staff members of the Atlanta Historical Society were especially helpful: Franklin M. Garrett, Ted Ryan, Bill Hull, Helen Matthews, Frank Wheeler, Susan Barnard, Rosa Dickens, Jacque Kavanaugh, John Ott, and Anne Salter. Carole Merritt, director of the Herndon Home, helped with her expert knowledge of the black community; she referred me to Mrs. James D. Palmer, who put me in touch with Dr. Johnnetta Cole of Spelman College. I would also like to thank Anne Farrisee with the Atlanta Preservation Center and Philip Cheek with BellSouth.

Among architects and associates who helped were Norman Davenport Askins, Tom Collum, and Eugene L. Surber, all of Atlanta, and Jack R. Wilson of Moultrie, Georgia; and Dorothy Spence, executive director of the Georgia Chapter of the AIA in Atlanta; as well as Mrs. Clement J. Ford, wife of the architect Clem Ford. Two interior decorators should be thanked for their help: David Byers and Gordon Little. Those who shared neighborhood information, in addition to that provided by homeowners, were Mrs. Ivan Allen, Jr., Mrs. Jeremiah Luxemberger, Mrs. Matilda Martin Dobbs, Mr. Don Grady, Mr. Wesley Rhodes Vawter III, and Mr. Kenneth Thomas, Jr., who also assisted with data about districts on the National Register of Historic Places.

Jean Ann Keagle Brown and Louisa McIntosh, each, at various times in the preparation of the book, leased me temporary office space in my condominium building (at starving-artist rates). Lynne Smith and Wendy Anderson of Atlanta Document Services diligently did their part typing the manuscript. The Freemeyers, of the Minuteman Press in my building, were open long hours with their phalanx of machines and helpful attitude.

In addition to the tremendous effort by Ted Ryan and Bill Hull at AHS, others who made significant contributions of time and expertise helping Van with the massive task of procuring illustrations were: Jim and Mary Lee Lockhart; Michael Siede; Susan Hunter of Graphics International; Martha Pacini and Kristen Bell of Heery International; Alice Stevens of John Portman and Associates; Lisa Simmons and Chuck Moody of Cousins Properties; and Gary Goettling at Georgia Tech.

Special thanks should be made to Margaret Quinlin, Jill Smith, Wayne Elliott, and the staff at Peachtree Publishers, who were involved in this project at its conception and put considerable time and resources into various stages of its development.

Providing invaluable assistance in constructing the finished product were several old comrades in arts: Lisa Lytton-Smith and Rusty Smith and David Kaminsky and Sarah Albertin at Savannah Color Services. Thanks also to George Dick, Bobbie Dean, and the staff at Four Colour Imports.

Special mention should be made of H. Paul St. Martin, who has joined the fray as co-publisher with Van in our attempt to help preserve the essence of our native South.

Constantly, as ever, my mother, Miriam Hays Mitchell—a native of Macon, a long-time resident of Atlanta, then Savannah, and now Atlanta again—cheerfully provided many kinds of help that allowed my work to proceed. Following *Classic Savannah*, this time I sought to record and define the persistent and historic principles and aspects, the classic spirit, animating the seemingly ever-evolving, phoenix-like metropolis of Atlanta.

ATLANTA HISTORICAL SOCIETY
COLLECTIONS

BIRD'S-EYE VIEW OF THE COTTON STATES AND INTERNATIONAL EXPOSITION==ATLANTA, GA., U.S.A.
OPENS SEPTEMBER 18th. CLOSES DECEMBER 31st
1895.

IN 1926, WHEN THE ATLANTA HISTORICAL SOCIETY was founded, the vision was to collect and preserve the history of the city. Today, that vision has grown to include two historic houses and a museum in addition to the library-archives, all actively engaged in collecting, interpreting and making available to the public the history of Atlanta.

The library-archives of the Atlanta Historical Society, located in McElreath Hall, contains more than nineteen thousand volumes of books, eight hundred manuscript collections, and more than one million photographs. The collections focus on the history of Atlanta with emphasis on the political and social aspects of the city's growth. Special collecting focus has emphasized materials relating to the Civil War, civil rights, and local history.

One of the most widely requested needs in the local history area has been material to document the structural history of the city—the buildings, houses, parks, and all elements that culminate in understanding a neighborhood's

history. With this need in mind, the Atlanta Historical Society has actively sought materials to improve collections in this area. Architectural drawings, maps, photographs, and property titles have been included in the collecting focus to assist the public with research requests. Currently, these include representative work from more than thirty architectural firms in the city, totaling thousands of individual drawings. Accompanying photographs are included with many of these projects.

The library-archives actively seeks donations of additional materials to add to its collections. The research room is open to the public and serves approximately five thousand patrons per year through reference services including letter, telephone, and personal inquiry. Photographic services and photocopy services are available.

The Atlanta Historical Society photographic collection was the source of almost all of the archival images used in *Classic Atlanta.*

"Plus ça change, plus c'est la même chose."
(The more things change, the more they remain the same.)
FRENCH PROVERB

IN 1988, FROM THE CUPOLA-LANTERN at the top of the gold dome of the state Capitol, we made this first photographic image for *Classic Atlanta*. We stood 237 feet above the base of the building, which sits on Capitol Square, the highest site in downtown Atlanta, 1,050 feet above sea level, 1,287 feet in all. The photograph was based on a panoramic view of Five Points, the historic center of the city, made from that same dizzying perch about 1915 for a large fold-out postcard that I have had for many years. The views from that somewhat precarious spot, made almost seventy-five years apart, would tell an instant story of things changing yet unchanging. The French proverb, roughly translated as, "The more things change, the more they remain the same," definitely applies to Atlanta. For, the more change, the more Atlanta embraces its potential. This Atlanta Spirit, a classic thing about the city, is fundamental, yet there are some other landmark aspects that seem to change little and remain constants of value.

Peachtree Ridge, over there at the Five Points crossroads, remains a granite-rock-solid landmark, the historic spine of the city from southwest to northeast. And many—

not all—of the early twentieth-century skyscrapers in that 1915 skyline view remain to let us know this is Atlanta. That we were photographing from atop the state Capitol (dedicated July 4, 1889) tells us we are in Atlanta, the 1868 replacement for Milledgeville as the capital of the state. To capture the first image for the book, from that high vantage, at that juncture seemed symbolic to me of the bold aspirations we had for the project.

I had first climbed to the very top of the Georgia Capitol dome to look over the city of my birth, when I was nine. Then it was also quite a breath-taking trek and view, but then I was not helping Van Martin haul many pounds of camera equipment up the spiraling staircase within the inner workings of a dome normally glimpsed today as one speeds by on I-75/85.

Van and I began the long climb through an inconspicuous side door into a storeroom that brought back memories. It had been the cozy office of a porter, a kindly, long-suffering gray-haired man who sometimes entertained me for my father, whom he helped with office chores; that porter first took me on the adventure to the very tip-top of the dome.

April 9, 1938, I had been born practically under the shadow of the Georgia Capitol dome—then not gilded as it is now—in a private hospital no longer located there. My father's office was in the capitol. Its classical dome and soaring columned interior—the monumental architecture of it all—first piqued my curiosity about the fine art of buildings, inspired me to want to understand how they came to be. After my father and mother married in Macon, they had come to Atlanta for him to attend college and to clerk in the state comptroller-general's office; that officer's main responsibility was the state insurance commission. By the time I first made it to the top to look out from the cupola-lantern, Governor Ellis Arnall had appointed my father Comptroller General-Insurance Commissioner, so I guess that meant I was finally entitled to the run of the place. (Later, I served as a page in the State Senate, and still later, to return the favor, I proposed the building as a National Historic Landmark, a status it attained in the mid-1970s.)

Capitol derives from Latin *Capitolium*. Professor Mircea Eliade says that a domed capitol building is a "universe in miniature." He says that each of us has a "nostalgia for origins" and a desire to be "at the center of the world." As a child when I looked up from the marble floor of the rotunda, and even now, I feel that in that place I am at the center of a known universe. A domed building, for Eliade, "copies the cosmos," is a "ceremonial house." The dome symbolizes heaven, and the four walls are the four points of the compass, the four horizons. The cupola-lantern, which sits above the rotunda and above the dome, is an eye to the world and the heavens.

A view from the top of that dome was the way I wanted to begin this book. My little moment in the sun in 1946–47, when my father's office had been in the capitol, helped me and Van Martin obtain the key to the locked-up stairway. The security guard figured I was okay because I had climbed up there before; I had origins in that state house.

In January 1989 I only sat at 950 feet elevation, however, at 1421 Peachtree Street, N.E., Ansley Park, in the sector of the city since 1972 called Midtown, when I wrote the introduction, "The Atlanta Spirit." That office-residence is near where I had once lived for many years and where my father's insurance business had been located, on Peachtree near Fourteenth Street, for twenty-five years after, as he would say, he "left the Capitol."

From birth, knowing this place, first called Atlanta in 1845, I knew that the city has a mythology classic in its

Views from the cupola-lantern atop the Capitol dome. Opposite: 1988. Above: 1903.

simplicity, as a mythology should be, so that everyone can grasp the story. This story is of the rebirth and persistence of the Phoenix: the legendary Egyptian bird that rises from the ashes, unconsumed, to live another life, able to rise to new heights, boundless, striving, restless, and always unfinished. This legend became part of the city seal in 1887.

Can this mythology of city building and rebuilding, which has traditionally inspired Atlanta, have a "cease-fire" long enough to make a place in which to rest peacefully under its famous green canopy of trees spreading over the beautiful piedmont terrain as far as the eye can see? Must we always be reduced to ashes, as in 1864, only to rebuild bigger and higher? Can we not preserve something of our past as part of our spreading horizons. These now stretch farther and farther from such landmarks of the Atlanta Spirit as the historic capitol in the center of the old downtown where Terminus was conceived and the Zero Mile Post was driven into the red clay. Can there be a new Phoenix that protects the old nest rather than destroying it every other generation; a bird that stays home to fix up the place; make it even more beautiful and comfortable; tending its own garden, and attending neighborhood civic association meetings? There is evidence in this book that the Atlanta Phoenix can and does.

While I was working on the text, Lewis Mumford (1895-1990), one of my cultural heros, died, and I reread his *The City in History* (1961), which has been called the greatest book ever written on the city. Mumford, who loved "neighborhood-centered cities", wrote: "City after city has taken mere physical and economic expansion as a testimony to its prosperity and culture." Mumford wrote: "The city is an agent of human continuity." He quoted Emerson, "The city lives by remembering."

Because the Atlanta Spirit is one of hope and persistence, let us persist in hoping that the more Atlanta changes, the more it remains a good place in which to "hold these truths to be self-evident, That all men [persons] are created equal; that they are endowed by their creator with certain unalienable rights; that among these are life, liberty, and the pursuit of happiness; . . ." That Jeffersonian American dream must persist for every generation; and citizens must send legislators to sit under landmark domes who would not let that spirit perish from this earth.

William R. Mitchell, Jr.
Atlanta, 1991

The
Atlanta Spirit

Atlanta, the Gate City . . . between the Atlantic and the West, is a grand type of progress, bounding, alert, prolific, irresistible. She is up to the most advanced ideas of the age. She represents emphatically the new and modern Georgia, made up of all types, ideas, and nationalities, fused into one vital, resolute, outstanding concentration of power and growth.

I. W. Avery

ATLANTA IN THE EMPIRE STATE OF THE SOUTH, 1885

IN 1990, THE ATLANTA METROPOLITAN STATISTICAL AREA (MSA) consisted of eighteen counties, inhabited by an estimated 2,833,511 people. Two of the counties, Cobb and Gwinnett, have recently vied for the title of fastest-growing county in the United States, and the Atlanta metropolitan area is one of the top dozen urban concentrations of people in North America—and the largest in the Southeast. That has not always been the case. But, as journalist I. W. Avery said in 1885, Atlanta progress is "irresistible." Irresistible, indeed, as the statistics show.

In the 1830s, the Atlanta Metropolitan Statistical Area of today was the northern frontier of white expansion in Georgia, and most of the counties in the MSA had not even been created. (Fulton, now the home county of the City of Atlanta, was not defined until 1853.) In 1837, when Atlanta began as a frontier railroad terminus for the Western and Atlantic Railroad, the nearest settlement stood in Dekalb County—formed in 1822, of which Decatur was and is the county seat. In fact, the camp that grew up around the railroad was originally

called "Terminus," then Marthasville. Not until 1845 was Marthasville christened Atlanta—a coinage derived from the Atlantic in "Western and Atlantic." Incorporated in 1847, the town became the City of Atlanta and started out with corporate limits extending one mile in every direction from the state railroad depot that stood near the present-day capitol.

Classic Atlanta is about how that circular village on the north Georgia frontier—then only recently ceded by the Creek Nation—grew into one of the largest and fastest-growing metropolitan areas in the United States. What sort of place has it been and has it become? What is "classic Atlanta?" What is the spirit—or *genius loci*, as the ancients put it—of this irresistible place with the classical-sounding name of Atlanta? What is the genius of this place?

The first street directory was published in 1859, when the population of Atlanta had reached 7,500 and Fulton County an additional 3,800. An attorney, Greene B. Haygood, wrote the foreword in which he said what people have been saying ever since: "The population of the city is remarkable for its

Opposite page: View of the downtown skyline from atop the State Archives Building in the winter of 1991. Above: The Capitol rose above the surrounding city in 1895.

activity and enterprise." A few years later, in 1866, only two years after the utter destruction that occurred during the last summer of the Civil War, Whitelaw Reid, a New York journalist, passed through and later reported: "The people of Atlanta were infected with the mania of city building." By the time Whitelaw Reid observed the recovering city, the classic enterprising spirit of Atlanta was well formed. It remains constant to this day, but some feel that the spirit of city building—as well as city "de-construction"—is too determined, too successfully consistent, perhaps too businesslike, and without due regard for quality of life.

In 1885, however, Atlanta lawyer, journalist, and historian, I. W. Avery, a former Confederate colonel turned city booster, had no reservations as he gave classic form to the legend of the Atlanta spirit. Avery wrote: "Atlanta exemplified the fable of the Phoenix. The regeneration was something miraculous. Like magic the imperial spirit of the city asserted its life. . . . From the baptism of ashes arose the present magnificent ideal of a city."

In 1887, when Atlanta celebrated the fiftieth anniversary of its founding, the city officially adopted the phoenix and the latin motto *Resurgens,* "rising again," for a city seal that is still used. This tradition of city-building, of optimism and determinism, which the seal represents, a tradition of rebirth that has often taken on an almost religious character, is the mythology of Atlanta, and goes a long way in helping to explain the *genius loci.*

As Atlantans forged a metropolis from a wilderness rail-road terminus, however, and the "present magnificent ideal of a city" began its rise, something of its wilderness character survived in suburban residential areas of great natural and manmade beauty. This too was part of the Atlanta spirit, the genius of the place. In 1942 the American Guide Series book on Atlanta reported: "Atlanta is renowned for the taste and sumptuousness of its residences in a green setting of trees, shrubbery and sweeping hills. . . . Yet this notable architecture has developed from an origin of pioneer crudeness within a century."

Thus by the 1940s the beauty of the Atlanta residential suburbs had gained national renown, and a large part of that reputation has always been attributed to the influence of one architect, Neel Reid (1885–1926), of the firm of Hentz, Reid & Adler. Yet there were many other architects and well-informed clients who helped give form to what the Atlanta spirit required in houses and other buildings that constitute the bricks-and-mortar of a city.

In reality, at the time of Neel Reid's birth in 1885, the Atlanta spirit was already working its magic on the rolling and wooded north Georgia topography, but the skyscrapers that had begun to rise at Five Points in the center of downtown were not its only expressions. Atlantans were busy, but not all business. In a publication distributed at the Chicago Exposition of 1893, I. W. Avery reported: "Atlanta is the hub of an immense wheel of magnificent and thriving suburbs with beautiful streets of homes and churches." True to the Atlanta spirit, the Old South colonel turned New South journalist did

Introduction: The Atlanta Spirit

not mind tooting a horn. ("It has been said that every citizen of Atlanta carries a horn with him and blows it on all occasions," observed William Lowndes Calhoun in 1902.)

One of the suburbs to which Avery referred was Inman Park, the first planned neighborhood in Atlanta. City-builder Joel Hurt laid out Inman Park in the late 1880s one-and-one-half miles east of the brand new state capitol, patterning the suburb after gardenesque villages such as Riverside, designed by Frederick Law Olmsted in Chicago. In the February 26, 1890, issue of the *Atlanta Constitution* Joel Hurt was quoted: "All that art and money can do has been done to make [Inman Park] a perfect place of residence." Hurt saved a magazine article from 1891 in his Inman Park scrapbook, which caught the Atlanta spirit in relation to suburbs: "Atlanta's habit is to lead in every line, and having gone extensively into the suburban business, she was bound to have the loveliest residential sections."

The dream was becoming a reality by 1902, when Atlanta historian Thomas H. Martin wrote: "Few cities in any part of the United States can show more attractive residence streets or architectural designs." Martin added, "Atlanta is a city of home owners." As Atlanta has grown in size and population, Atlantans have essentially remained true to Martin's turn-of-the-century observations. Many of the finest neighborhoods developed in the Atlanta area in the first half of the twentieth century, the older in-town neighborhoods such as Inman Park, Ansley Park, and Druid Hills in northeast Atlanta and those in Buckhead in northwest Atlanta, have become more and more sought after and are within the city limits as set in the 1952 Plan of Improvement (essentially those of the City of Atlanta in 1990). These planned neighborhoods are a legacy of the Atlanta spirit that modern generations are enjoying anew, and, in many respects they are classic Atlanta—the embodiment of the Atlanta spirit in an otherwise ever-changing cityscape.

Peachtree Street, for example, from just north of Five Points for miles into the county was for many years almost entirely residential. But little evidence of that remains, except for several fine houses on Peachtree Road (the "street" changes to "road" at Palisades Road). The Randolph-Lucas house at 2494, N. W., served as a fictional landmark in Anne Rivers Siddons's best-selling *Peachtree Road*, published in 1988. It is one of the last and best.

During the Cotton States Exposition of 1895, which Atlanta boosters promoted to acquaint the world with the great potential of the Southern city, the *New York Observer* reported: "Atlanta's private residences will compare with those of any city. Some of her merchant princes and professional men own fine houses on Peachtree Street and the adjacent thoroughfares. There are other avenues which in time will share

Springvale Park was a distinguishing feature of Inman Park in 1895.

the palm with Peachtree Street, but for the present that is the street." The palm began to pass to "adjacent thoroughfares" around 1905 when automobiles began to make the suburbs even more accessible than the excellent system of street railways had in the last quarter of the nineteenth century. The Atlanta spirit began to settle permanently into garden suburbs such as Ansley Park in single-family dwellings surrounded by landscaped grounds, rather than in rowhouses or in apartment buildings, which were never as popular in Atlanta as in other cities. (Bungalows were the rowhouses of Atlanta.)

Perhaps the classic statement of the Atlanta spirit at its most zealous was made in 1905 by an Atlanta native who had grown up on Peachtree Street just north of Five Points and became one of the earliest settlers in the suburban Buckhead section. The banker Robert Foster Maddox (1870-1965), who served as mayor in 1909 and 1910, was president of the chamber of commerce in 1905 when he made his final speech; Maddox spoke as though repeating a creed his audience would join into as a hymn, the classic old story of their faith:

"The 'Atlanta Spirit' was conceived in the time of Terminus, born in Marthasville, suffered under the fire of Sherman, but rose again from the ashes of war to lead us with its white light through the dark days of reconstruction, and has since illuminated the way for a brave and generous people, with ready hands and willing hearts to build a great city."

"To build a great city" has been the Atlanta spirit—the genius of the place—from the first. This ambition is not as indigenous as some of the other Southern mythologies, but it is not a Yankee malady only. Atlanta is proof of that.

Margaret Mitchell, whose pen helped to put Atlanta on the world map in the 1930s and was a certified Southerner, put it this way in *Gone With the Wind*: "The people who settled the town . . . were a pushy people. Restless, energetic people. . . . They were proud of the place, proud of its growth, proud of themselves for making it grow."

In 1959 Ralph McGill, well-known editor of the *Atlanta Constitution*, caught the spirit in this way: "Atlanta was born with energy in her body. In her genes were transportation, movement, drive." One of McGill's successors, Reg Murphy, wrote in 1970: "Somebody has called Atlanta a 'city of optimists.'"

Each generation has sensed essentially the same spirit, but perhaps has become more prosaic in expressing it. Some have become cooler and ironic, often adding a touch of ridicule for so old-fashioned an idea as the faith of one's forefathers in "city building"—as though the biblical "Pride goeth before destruction, and a haughty spirit before a fall" is what it had all been about. Atlanta had just been committing hubris—"exaggerated pride of self-confidence often resulting in retribution." No rebirth allowed!

Not that all along some had not warned of exaggerated pride. Journalist Rebecca Latimer Felton (1835–1930), the first woman to have a seat in the U. S. Senate, said in 1885, and none too kindly: "In our opinion Atlanta succeeds by her 'cheek' and supreme confidence in herself." Historian U. B. Phillips commented in 1908: "The unbounded ambition for their town, and their clamor of self-advertisement hastened her growth." Margaret Mitchell herself had described Atlantans as "pushy." And practically everyone has heard some variation of: "If Atlanta could suck as hard as it can blow, the Atlantic Ocean would be at the State Capitol!"

In the 1980s, during its anniversary of 150 years, the city received a *coup de grace* a day from some national commentator. In 1987 Arthur Frommer, the tourist-business expert famous for *Europe on Five Dollars a Day*, told an Atlanta audience that their beloved city was indeed big, well served by airlines and hotels, yes, and a business success, but a bore around which no one wanted to linger. The worst "press" of all, perhaps, came from a business journalist in the *Wall Street Journal* only a few months before the Democratic National Convention was held in Atlanta during the summer of 1988; John Helyar wrote February 29, 1988: "Greater Atlanta has come to bestride the region through . . . the sheer force of boosterism. If New York is the Big Apple and New Orleans the Big Easy, Atlanta is the Big Hustle."

The "Big Hustle" could mean several things, of course, but it sounds a great deal less kind than James Street's famous remarks in *Holiday* magazine in January 1951: "Atlanta means roughly the same as Atlantic, but she's about 200 miles from the ocean and doing all right for a mountain gal. Her patron saint is Scarlett O'Hara, and the town's just like her—shrewd, proud and full of gumption, her Confederate slip showing under a Yankee mink coat." Hustle can mean "to obtain by energetic activity," to "sell something to or obtain something from by energetic and especially underhanded activity," to "make strenuous efforts to secure money or business," or to "obtain money by fraud or deception." And, it can mean to "engage in prostitution."

Greene B. Haygood in 1859 did say that Atlanta ceased to be called Marthasville because some thought the "bustling village, the embryo city . . . had become too fast, too gross,

too great and too pretentious to wear any longer, with maidenly modesty, the name of its fair matronymic."

Even local political writers sniped, as Bill Shipp did in January 1989: "Let's be honest, Atlanta never was the world's next great city. It just thought it was. Still thinks it is." One of the unkindest cuts came in a January 9, 1989, *New Yorker* article entitled "The Malady of Gigantism" by writer Brendan Gill: "Atlanta is a boomtown that has gone on booming; the not very old 'old' Atlanta has yielded to a new and amorphous megAtlanta."

Has success spoiled Atlanta? Some definitely seem to think so. This book, however, believes in the classic Atlanta myth of the phoenix; believes the Atlanta spirit will prevail, and a twenty-first-century Atlanta will emerge reinvigorated from the flames of the twentieth-century strivings that follow in the footsteps of a whole host of Atlanta forefathers.

It is classic and within the spirit to think that Atlanta has not really gone down for the "ten count," but will come back as refreshed as a drink of her favorite cola. Asa Griggs Candler, who first put Coca-Cola, and thereby Atlanta, on the map of the world, once said: "The dawn of a greater Atlanta is at hand, the spirit and influence of which will spread across a horizon as yet undreamed of." Atlanta has been the home of Asa Candler's and Robert Woodruff's Coca-Cola (now called Classic); of Joel Chandler Harris's Uncle Remus; of Margaret Mitchell's *Gone With the Wind*; of Bobby Jones, the greatest golf champion of all; of John Portman, a new kind of architect-developer; of Martin Luther King, Jr., the Nobel prize-winning civil rights leader; of former President Jimmy Carter's library and center; and of Ted Turner's broadcasting empire. These reputations are not to be undervalued as new worlds are conquered.

The IBM building towers above Winn Park and the Midtown neighborhood of Ansley Park in 1990.

Recall, if you please, that Atlanta and Scarlett O'Hara were christened in the same year of 1845, and Scarlett has lived on in the eternal impetuous optimism of her youth, rediscovered by every generation. Recall the hosanna on which her story closed, "With the spirit of her people who would not know defeat, even when it stared them in the face, she raised her chin. . . . After all, tomorrow is another day."

That is the classic Atlanta spirit—the American dream set in the Deep South, a story not yet over.

PANORAMA VIEW OF ATLANTA, GA.
"THE METROPOLIS OF THE NEW SOUTH."

Kimball Hotel   Atlanta National Bank   Fourth National Bank Building   Third National Bank Building   Empire Building

The Atlanta Spirit in Architecture

One of the first impressions of surprise that a newcomer receives here is from the number and size of the skyscrapers. Atlanta has more office buildings than any other city of its size in the world. They and the lofty hotels give to Atlanta a skyline which has astonished very many people. It is the skyline of a true metropolis. In a word Atlanta is the leading city in the progress of the South.

Caption from a c. 1915 postcard

Building   Healy Building   Empire Life Building   Forsyth Building   Piedmont Hotel   Hotel Ansley   Candler Building

IN A RELATIVELY SHORT SPAN OF TIME, Atlanta, which had its origin in the humble setting of a frontier railroad camp, has blossomed into the largest and most famous city of the South. This spectacular growth—the building up, pulling down, and then rebuilding ever more ambitiously—has created several "Atlantas" in 150 years. While this delights real estate interests and intrigues historians, it frustrates historic preservationists. Atlanta was founded as an inland railroad terminus in 1837, as the industrial revolution gathered steam. Architectural revivalism and eclecticism—almost always constants in Atlanta—were becoming the fashion, and it was just at the beginning of the

era of professional architects. After the Civil War, the famous Atlanta "rise from the ashes" created opportunities for architects and related professions, and that has never ceased. In 1908 a school of architecture was established at the Georgia Institute of Technology (Georgia Tech); this came at an opportune time to provide professional training as the city brought into the twentieth century its aspirations of achieving primacy in the region and the nation.

This irrepressible Atlanta spirit of growth and destiny has often been thought to be more Yankee than Southern. Yet it does occur in the deep South, and conservative social values—decorum, formality, and tradition—

have been underlying rules of taste not only in the domestic life of the city, but also in her architecture. Here, in the form of an illustrated timeline, are images and observations that represent landmarks in the remarkable history of the hard-charging, ever-changing "Gate City of the South."

Above: A panorama of the Atlanta skyline about 1915 illustrates the impact of one of the city's most prolonged and significant building booms—the years immediately before and the two decades following the 1895 Cotton States and International Cotton Exposition. One of the oldest survivors of that era is the 1897 Empire Life (Flatiron) Building.

Atlanta Timeline

1733   Georgia founded as thirteenth British colony; first settlement established at Savannah.

1814   Fort Peachtree (or Gilmer) built on the north Georgia frontier, on the east bank of the Chattahoochee River at Peachtree Creek.

1823   Decatur and Dekalb County founded.

1832   Marietta and Cobb County founded.

1833   Arrival of Hardy Ivy, first white settler at the future site of Atlanta.

1835   White Hall Tavern built at the future site of West End.

1837   Southern terminus of the state-chartered Western and Atlantic Railroad in Land Lot 78, Dekalb County, established the locus of the future city center; first settlement called, appropriately, "Terminus."

Map of Marthasville, c. 1845. [18.1]

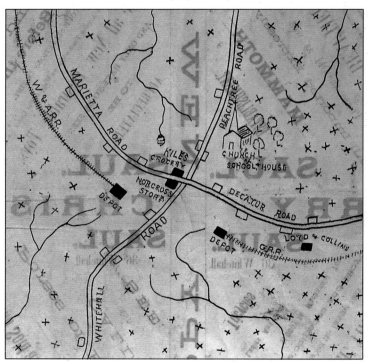

1838   Roswell founded by Roswell King.

Henry Irby of South Carolina erected tavern-grocery store at the intersection of Peachtree and Roswell roads at the place that came to be called Buckhead.

1842   Exact center of "Terminus" relocated to present site of Zero Mile Post in Land Lot 77.

1843   Settlement of "Terminus" incorporated as town of Marthasville.

1845   Georgia Railroad line from Augusta completed.

All the railroads [in the Southeast] must necessarily unite at a point in Dekalb County, Georgia, called Atlanta, not far from Decatur.
  John C. Calhoun
  Memphis, Tennessee, 1845

Town of Marthasville renamed Atlanta, a coinage based on the word Atlantic.

1846   Macon and Western (now the Central of Georgia) Railroad completed.

1847   City of Atlanta incorporated with circular city limits.

1850   Population: 2,569.

Zero Mile Post erected at site established in 1842; the post, the oldest man-made Atlanta landmark, still stands at the original site, now part of Underground Atlanta; original city limits extended in a one-mile radius from this point.

After many delays, the Western and Atlantic Railroad finally began through service between Chattanooga and Atlanta.

Six-acre city cemetery (later named Oakland) established.

Western and Atlantic bridge across the Chattahoochee River. [19.1]

1852   John Boutell (1814-1886), a Massachusetts native and possibly the first architect in Atlanta, erected his home north of the center of town, just off Peachtree Street.

1853   Atlanta became the county seat of newly created Fulton County. [19.2]

Atlanta City Hall-Fulton County Courthouse and square, 1854, with Second Baptist and Central Presbyterian churches and the spires of the Shrine of the Immaculate Conception. [19.2]

1854   First city seal adopted. [19.3]

1854 city seal. [19.3]

1856   Atlanta Gas Light Company incorporated.

1857   Atlanta called the "Gate City" at celebration marking the completion of the Memphis and Charleston Railway.

1859   First city directory published with "Sketch of Atlanta" by Greene B. Haygood, Esq.

The population of the city is remarkable for its activity and enterprise. Most of the inhabitants came here for the purpose of bettering their fortunes.
   Greene B. Haygood
   "Sketch of Atlanta," 1859

1860   Population: 7,741 (total Fulton County population: 11,572).

Judge Clark Howell (1811-1882) established Howell's Mill on Peachtree Creek.

1861   Civil War began; President Jefferson Davis, CSA, visited Atlanta on his way to Montgomery, Alabama.

1862   Atlanta became an important Confederate city as a large supply base and workshop for war materials and a hospital and relief center.

1863   Colonel Lemuel P. Grant, CSA, began building elaborate defenses around the perimeter of the city.

Rail yard after the city was burned. [19.4]

1864   May 8, General William Tecumseh Sherman launched the Atlanta Campaign at Dalton; July 22, Battle of Atlanta, one of four principal engagements for possession of the city; September 2, city surrendered; night of November 14, the city was burned, and the next morning Sherman began the March to the Sea.

1865   Civil War ended.

1866   City limits extended 1.5 miles in a circle from Zero Mile Post.

The people of Atlanta were infected with the mania of city-building.
Whitelaw Reid
AFTER THE WAR, 1866

1867   Atlanta University chartered.

Kimball's Opera House. [20.1]

1868   Atlanta chosen as the new state capital; Kimball's Opera House became the first capitol building. [20.1]

Atlanta is certainly a fast place in every sense of the word, and our friends in Atlanta are fast people. . . . To a stranger the whole city seems to be running on wheels, and all the inhabitants continually blowing off steam.

Editor
MILLEDGEVILLE FEDERAL UNION
February 12, 1867

West End incorporated.

Atlanta Constitution incorporated.

Shrine of the Immaculate Conception. [20.2]

1869   Shrine of the Immaculate Conception begun, Wlliam H. Parkins (1836-1894), architect. [20.2]

1870   Population: 21,789.

Hannibal I. Kimball, a native of Maine, erected Kimball House hotel. [20.3]

First Kimball House hotel, 1870. [20.3]

1871   Chamber of Commerce organized.

1872   Reconstruction effectively ended in Atlanta.

1874   New city charter approved; power of mayor increased.

Henry Grady, *Atlanta Constitution* editor, wrote of the "New South" for the first time.

1875   Joel Hurt arrived in Atlanta.

1876   City cemetery named Oakland Cemetery.

1877   First telephone service in Atlanta.

United States Post Office and Custom House, 1878. [21.1]

Southern Bell Telephone Company, 1881. [21.3]

1878 United States Post Office and Custom House built at Five Points on Marietta Street (building became Atlanta City Hall in 1910). [21.1]

E. Y. Clarke published *Illustrated History of Atlanta.*

1879 Thomas H. Morgan (1857–1940), architect, came to Atlanta.

Alexander C. Bruce (1835–1927), architect, came to Atlanta.

1880 Population: 37,409.

1881 Joel Chandler Harris moved into "Wren's Nest" in West End.

Southern Bell Telephone Company established Atlanta office. [21.3]

1882 Col. L. P. Grant offered Atlanta 100 acres for Grant Park in southeast quadrant.

Fulton County Courthouse, 1883. [21.4]

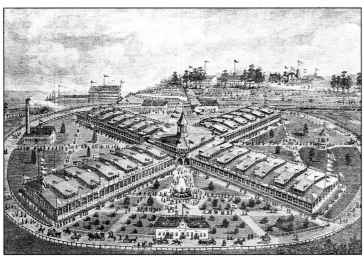

1881 International Cotton Exposition. [21.2]

International Cotton Exposition held, the first of several industrial fairs. [21.2]

1883 Fulton County Courthouse completed (torn down in 1911). [21.4]

The Atlanta Spirit in Architecture

1883   State legislature appropriated $1,000,000 for state capitol.

Kimball House burned.

H. M. Patterson opened funeral home.

Capital City Club chartered.

Edward C. Peters house built; the architect, Gottfried L. Norrman (1846–1909), had come to Atlanta to design several structures for the 1881 cotton exposition.

1884   Peters' Park subdivision conceived west of Peachtree Street along North Avenue.

First interment at West View Cemetery.

Central Presbyterian Church built at 201 Washington Street, E. G. Lind, architect.

In our opinion Atlanta succeeds by her "cheek" and supreme confidence in herself.
Rebecca Latimer Felton, 1885

Second Kimball House, 1885. [22.1]

1885   Second Kimball House built. [22.1]

Georgia Institute of Technology founded.

Baltimore Block, the first rowhouses in Atlanta, constructed just north of downtown.

Atlanta has exemplified the fable of the Phoenix. The regeneration was something miraculous. Like magic the imperial spirit of the city asserted its life. . . . From the baptism of ashes arose the present magnificent ideal of a city.
I. W. Avery
THE PHOENIX OF THE SOUTH, 1885

1886   Coca-Cola originated by Dr. John Pemberton.

Joel Hurt formed East Atlanta Land Company to develop Inman Park, the Atlanta and Edgewood (electric) Street Railway Company, and the Equitable Building.

Henry Grady gave "The New South" speech in New York City.

I want to say to General Sherman . . . that from the ashes he left us in 1864 we have raised a brave and beautiful city; that somehow or other we have caught the sunshine in the bricks and mortar of our homes.
Henry W. Grady
"The New South," 1886

Second (and current) city seal, 1887. [22.2]

1887   City Seal adopted with the phoenix as the symbol and *Resurgens* as the motto. [22.2]

1887 Piedmont Cotton Exposition. [23.1]

Piedmont Cotton Exposition held at what is now Piedmont Park. [23.1]

"The New South" supplement on Atlanta appeared in *Harper's Weekly* .

The Gentleman's—now Piedmont—Driving Club organized.

1888 Asa G. Candler acquired control of Coca-Cola Company.

Atlanta has every appearance of being the legitimate offspring of Chicago. There is nothing of the Old South about it, and all the traditions of the old-time South . . . have no place in the men of the present in the young and thriving Gate City.
A. K. McClure
Philadelphia, c. 1887

Georgia Capitol building, 1889. [23.3]

1889 New capitol completed, Edbrooke & Burnham of Chicago, architects. [23.3]

Henry Grady died.

Agnes Scott College established in Decatur. [24.1]

Fort McPherson established in southwest Atlanta. [24.2]

Hebrew Orphans' Home, 1888. [23.2]

Hebrew Orphans' Home built at 478 Washington Street, G. L. Norrman, architect. [23.2]

The Atlanta Spirit in Architecture

Agnes Scott College, 1889. [24.1]

Ft. McPherson, 1889. [24.2]

Henry Grady statue, 1891. [24.3]

1890   Population: 65,533.

Frederick Law Olmsted, landscape architect, visited Atlanta at the invitation of Joel Hurt.

1891   Henry Grady memorial statue unveiled at Five Points. [24.3]

Big Bethel African Methodist Episcopal Church begun on Auburn Avenue. Completed in 1921, gutted by fire in 1923, and rebuilt in 1924. [24.4]

1892   Equitable Building completed at Pryor and Edgewood, John Wellborn Root (1850–1891), architect. [24.5]

Big Bethel A. M. E. Church, 1891. [24.4]

Equitable Building, 1892. [24.5]

Aragon Hotel, 1892. [25.1]

Aragon Hotel built at Peachtree and Ellis streets. [25.1]

William Greene Raoul house built at 848 Peachtree Street, Bradford L. Gilbert of New York, architect.

1893 Frederick Law Olmsted came to Atlanta to help Joel Hurt plan the suburban area that came to be called Druid Hills.

1894 West End absorbed into Atlanta as the Seventh Ward.

Cotton States and International Exposition, 1895. [25.2]

1895 Cotton States and International Exposition held in Piedmont Park. [25.2]

1896 Golf first played in Atlanta when the Piedmont Driving Club laid out a short course (later absorbed into Piedmont Park).

"Flatiron" Building, 1896. [25.3]

English-American ("Flatiron") Building built at 74 Peachtree Street, Bradford Gilbert, architect, New York. [25.3]

Sacred Heart Church, 1897. [25.4]

1897 Sacred Heart Church built on Peachtree Street at Ivy, W. T. Downing, architect. [25.4]

1898 Prudential (Grant) Building built at 44 Broad Street, Bruce & Morgan, architects; early office skyscraper. [26.1]

William A. Wimbish house (now Atlanta Women's Club), built at 1150 Peachtree Street, W. T. Downing architect.

Prudential (Grant) Building, 1898. [26.1]

North Ave. Presbyterian Church, 1901. [26.3]

Carnegie Library, 1899. [26.2]

1899 Carnegie Library of Atlanta organized; architectural competition for the design of the building held; winner was New York City firm of Ackerman and Ross; Atlanta architects W. F. Denny and W. T. Downing won second and third places, respectively (building razed in 1980). [26.2]

1900 Population: 89,872.

1901 North Avenue Presbyterian Church built at 607 Peachtree Street, Bruce & Morgan, architects. [26.3]

The Empire Building completed at Broad and Marietta streets (remodeled in 1929 for the Citizens and Southern Bank). [26.4]

1902 Federal Penitentiary built at 601 McDonough Boulevard, Eames and Young, architects. [26.5]

Empire Building., 1901. [26.4]

Federal Penitentiary, 1902. [26.5]

Piedmont Hotel, 1903. [27.1]

1903 Piedmont Hotel, called "our New York hotel," built at Peachtree and Luckie streets, north of Five Points. [27.1]

James L. Dickey, Sr. (1847–1910), bought 405 acres on Paces Ferry Road, where he would later build his home.

1904 Ansley Park, originally called Peachtree Garden, planned and begun by E. P. Ansley.

A. G. Rhodes house (W. F. Denny, architect), built at 1516 Peachtree Street on the western edge of Ansley Park.

Robert Foster Maddox bought 73 acres of the Dickey property on the north side of Paces Ferry Road (now the site of the Governor's Mansion).

First movie shown in Atlanta.

It has been said that every citizen of Atlanta carries a horn with him and blows it on all occasions.
William Lowndes Calhoun
PIONEER CITIZENS OF ATLANTA, 1902

Third and Fourth National Banks. [27.2]

1905 Fourth National (later First National) Bank completed skyscraper office building at Five Points. [27.2]

Olmsted Brothers presented Joel Hurt the general plan for Druid Hills based on Frederick Law Olmsted's work.

The "Atlanta Spirit" was conceived in the time of Terminus, born in Marthasville, suffered under the fire of Sherman but rose again from the ashes of war to lead us with its white light through the dark days of reconstruction, and has since illumined the way for a brave and generous people, with ready hands and willing hearts to build a great city.
Robert F. Maddox
"President's Report,"
Atlanta Chamber of Commerce, 1905

The Atlanta Spirit in Architecture

Terminal Station, 1905. [28.1]

1905   Atlanta Terminal Station built at Spring Street, P. Thornton Marye, architect (building demolished in 1972). [28.1]

Atlanta Life Insurance Company founded.

1906   All Saints Episcopal Church, featuring seven stained glass windows by Tiffany Studios of New York City, built at 634 West Peachtree Street, Bruce and Morgan, architects.

St. Luke's Episcopal Church built at 435 Peachtree Street, P. Thornton Marye, architect.

Candler Building, a seventeen-story office building designed and built by George E. Murphy for Asa G. Candler, constructed on Peachtree Street north of Five Points. [28.2]

1908   Druid Hills sold by Joel Hurt to Asa Candler, who completed the suburb as originally planned by Olmsted and his sons.

Atlanta . . . resembles a Northern business city in the number of "skyscrapers" which have gone up within recent years, each of them a great hive of industry. It is different in this respect from any other city in the South. . . . In Atlanta all has gone; the old everywhere has made way for the new.

Charles Morris
THE OLD SOUTH AND THE NEW, 1907

Candler Building, 1906. [28.2]

School of Architecture begun at Georgia Institute of Technology.

The unbounded ambition of the people for their town, and their clamor of self-advertisement hastened her growth.

U. B. Phillips
TRANSPORTATION IN THE EASTERN COTTON BELT, 1908

1909   Atlanta had 1,300 "horseless carriages."

Hentz & Reid architectural firm formed.

Robert Foster Maddox (1870–1965) elected mayor of Atlanta.

West End Park, a bungalow suburb, begun south of West End business section.

Plaza Plan announced for covering downtown railroad gulch, Haralson Bleckley, architect. (Plan was never executed.) [29.1]

1910   Population: 154,839.

Design for the Plaza, 1909. [29.1]

Brookhaven Country Club organized (opened in 1911, merged with Capitol City Club in 1913).

Peachtree Heights Park formed, with Peachtree Battle Avenue and Habersham Road as major streets.

Alonzo Herndon mansion built at 587 University Place.

The Castle (Fort Peace) built by Ferdinand McMillan at 87 Fifteenth Street.

1911   Georgian Terrace Hotel built at Peachtree Street and Ponce de Leon Avenue, W. L. Stoddart, architect. [29.2]

Georgian Terrace Hotel, 1911. [29.2]

Capital City Club, 1911. [29.3]

Capital City Club built at 7 Harris Street, Donn Barber, architect. [29.3]

Post Office Building constructed at 56 Forsyth Street, John Knox Taylor, architect; now U. S. Court of Appeals.

Tuxedo Park Company organized; bought Dickey property in Buckhead.

1912   Philip Trammell Shutze (1890–1982) of Columbus, Georgia, graduated with a degree in architecture from Georgia Tech.

1913   Ponce de Leon Apartments built at Ponce de Leon Avenue at Peachtree Street, W. L. Stoddart, architect. [29.4]

Ponce de Leon Apartments, 1913. [29.4]

The Atlanta Spirit in Architecture

Panorama of Atlanta skyline, c. 1913. [30.1]

1913 Joel Chandler Harris Memorial Association acquired "Wren's Nest" in West End as a museum.

Asa G. Candler, president of the Coca-Cola Company, gave Emory College $1,000,000 to encourage the relocation of the campus from Oxford, Georgia, to Atlanta.

Healey Building, 1914. [30.2]

Hurt Building, 1914. [30.3]

1914 Healey Building built at 57 Forsyth Street, Bruce & Morgan, with W. T. Downing, architects. [30.2]

Hurt Building built at 45 Edgewood Avenue, J. E. R. Carpenter, architect. [30.3]

First Church of Christ. Scientist, 1914. [31.1]

First Church of Christ, Scientist built at 1235 Peachtree Street, Dougherty and Robinson, architects. [31.1]

Atlanta became the site of the Sixth District Federal Reserve Bank.

Fulton County Courthouse, 1915. [31.2]

1915   New Fulton County Courthouse completed at the southeast corner of Pryor and Hunter streets, A. Ten Eyck Brown and Morgan & Dillon, architects. [31.2]

Emory College rechartered as Emory University.

1916   Asa G. Candler built $210,000 mansion on Ponce de Leon Avenue in Druid Hills.

Neel Reid bought Mimosa Hall, a c. 1840 classical house in Roswell, and renovated it for his home.

1917   World War I began.

Peachtree Arcade, an enclosed shopping mall, built at Peachtree and Broad streets (demolished in 1964), A. Ten Eyck Brown, architect. [31.3]

Peachtree Arcade, 1917. [31.3]

1917   Asa G. Candler elected mayor.

Major fire along North Boulevard, Ponce de Leon Avenue, and North Avenue; 1,938 buildings on 300 acres destroyed.

1918   Brookwood Railroad Station built, Hentz, Reid & Adler, architects.

The Atlanta Spirit in Architecture

1919 Emory University opened in Druid Hills, Henry Hornbostel architect of campus plan and first buildings on quadrangle.

Candler family sells the Coca-Cola Company for $25,000,000 to Ernest Woodruff and his Trust Company of Georgia associates.

1920 Population: 200,616.

1921 Ebenezer Baptist Church, 413 Auburn Avenue, completed. [32.1]

Ebenezer Baptist Church, 1921. [32.1]

The Villa apartments built at 200 Montgomery Ferry Drive, Hentz, Reid & Adler, architects. [32.2]

The Villa Apartments, 1921. [32.2]

Howard Theatre, 1921. [32.3]

Howard Theater, designed by Hentz, Reid & Adler, was built on Peachtree Street for $1,000,000. (Later called the Paramount, it was demolished in 1965, but the facade was saved and incorporated in a residence built in south Georgia.) [32.3]

1922 City limits expanded on all sides, new wards created.

Town of Decatur became City of Decatur.

Brookwood Hills suburb began development.

WSB Radio, an Atlanta Journal project and the first commercial radio station in Atlanta, began broadcasting; WGST followed soon after.

The average Atlantan will not be satisfied, until it becomes one of the world's greatest centers of population . . . and is never quite so happy as when telling someone of its greatness.
   John R. Hornady
   ATLANTA, YESTERDAY, TODAY, AND TOMORROW, 1922

1923 Spring Street viaduct completed for $1,000,000, Robert & Company, architects and engineers.

Pershing Point developed with apartment buildings (now demolished for National Service Industries headquarters).

Brookhaven assigned a post office.

Rich's Department Store, 1923. [33.1]

Rich's Department Store built at 44 Broad Street, S.W., Hentz, Reid & Adler, architects. [33.1]

Ivey & Crook architectural firm formed from associates of Hentz, Reid & Adler.

Morningside Park began development.

Robert W. Woodruff (1889–1985) became president of the Coca Cola Company.

1924 Edwin P. Ansley's house in Ansley Park converted into governor's mansion (demolished in 1965).

Hurt Building enlarged eastward; became the largest office building in the South.

Biltmore Hotel, 1924. [33.2]

Biltmore Hotel, costing $6,000,000, opened, Leonard Schulze of New York, architect (closed in the early 1980s). [33.2]

Avondale Estates, adjoining Decatur, began development as Ingleside.

Davison's Department Store, 1925, and the Henry Grady Hotel, 1924. [33.3]

Henry Grady Hotel opened, G. Lloyd Preacher, architect. (On the site of former Peachtree Street governor's mansion, the hotel was demolished for the Westin International.) [33.3]

1925 City limits extended in all directions, including Morningside and Garden Hills.

Southern Railway began the deluxe Crescent Limited between New Orleans and New York, with a stop in Atlanta.

R. H. Macy's of New York and Davison-Paxon's of Atlanta announced merger and plans for a department store on the Peachtree Street site of the Richards-Abbott house, which was demolished; Starrett & Van Vleck of New York and Hentz, Reid & Adler of Atlanta, architects. [33.3]

Forward Atlanta Commission, a media campaign to make Atlanta more of a "branch office" town, established; chaired by Ivan Allen, Sr.

1926 Construction begun on Edward H. Inman (Swan) house at 3099 Andrews Drive, Hentz, Reid & Adler (later Hentz, Adler & Shutze), architects.

The Atlanta Spirit in Architecture

1926 Atlanta divided into four sectors: S.W., S.E., N.W., N.E., and all buildings renumbered according to a regular pattern, which is still used.

Asa G. Candler gave Candler Park on the southern border of Druid Hills and dedicated a golf course for the park.

Sears, Roebuck and Company began construction on its nine-story plant at 677 Ponce de Leon Avenue, Nimmons, Carr & Wright of Chicago, architects.

Atlanta Athletic Club moved into a new building downtown, Hentz, Reid & Adler, architects (building demolished in 1980).

Neel Reid died at Mimosa Hall in Roswell.

Cascade Heights developed, near historic Cascade Springs and south of West End.

Atlanta Historical Society chartered, Walter McElreath, first president.

High Museum of Art organized.

1927 Haynes Manor developed, west of Peachtree Heights Park along Peachtree Battle Avenue.

October 11, Charles A. Lindbergh Day in Atlanta; Lindbergh Drive named in his honor.

Hentz, Reid & Adler became Hentz, Adler & Shutze.

1928 Spring Hill Mortuary built at 1020 Spring Street, Hentz, Adler & Shutze, architects. [34.1]

Spring Hill Mortuary, 1928. [34.1]

Airmail service established between Atlanta and New York.

City limits extended eastward to include the town of East Lake.

City Hall, 1929. [34.2]

1929 New city hall, designed by G. Lloyd Preacher, built on the site of the old Girls' High School across from the capitol at 68 Mitchell Street. [34.2]

Martin Luther King, Jr., born January 15 at 501 Auburn Avenue.

Central Avenue and Pryor Street viaducts opened.

Rhodes Hall, 1516 Peachtree Street, preserved as the Georgia Department of Archives and History; the building is now the headquarters of the Georgia Trust for Historic Preservation and is undergoing restoration.

City of Atlanta purchased Candler Field (now Hartsfield Airport).

Rhodes-Haverty Building completed at 134 Peachtree Street, Pringle & Smith, architects; at 21 stories, the tallest office building in Atlanta at the time.

Southern Bell Headquarters, 1929. [35.1]

Headquarters for Southern Bell Telephone opened at 51 Ivy Street, Marye, Alger & Vinour, architects. [35.1]

Local banks merged to form First National Bank, one of the nation's largest banks.

First Baptist Church built at Peachtree Street between Fourth and Fifth streets, Burge & Stevens, architects. [35.2]

First Baptist Church, 1929. [35.2]

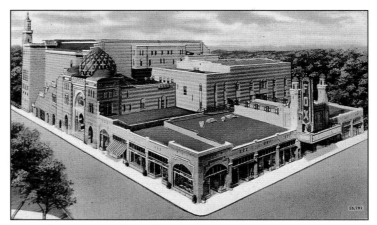

Fox Theatre, 1929. [35.3]

Fox Theater built at 660 Peachtree Street, Marye, Alger & Vinour, architects. (Now preserved by Atlanta Landmarks.) [35.3]

Atlanta University became the graduate school for Spelman and Morehouse colleges.

Bobby Jones and John A. White golf courses opened by the city.

1930 Population: 270,366 (within city limits); greater Atlanta population: 359,668.

William Oliver Building constructed at 32 Peachtree Street, Pringle & Smith, architects.

W. W. Orr Doctors' Building constructed at 490 Peachtree Street, Pringle & Smith, architects.

Union Depot opened, McDonald & Company, architects (demolished in 1970). [35.4]

Union Depot, 1930. [35.4]

The Atlanta Spirit in Architecture

1930 Bobby Jones completed his "Grand Slam" of the four most prestigious golfing events in the world; a homecoming parade was held in Atlanta; Jones later announced his retirement from tournament golf.

United States Post Office, 1931. [36.1]

1931 Post Office built at Forsyth, Hunter, and Spring streets, A. Ten Eyck Brown, architect. [36.1]

The Empire Building, built in 1901, remodeled by Citizens and Southern National Bank; Hentz, Adler & Shutze, architects.

Lenox Park subdivision planned by Ivey and Crook for Herbert Kaiser.

1932 Presidential candidate Franklin D. Roosevelt came to Atlanta to campaign.

Fulton County absorbed Campbell and Milton counties.

1933 To clear a slum area south of Georgia Tech the federal government began Techwood Homes, the first public housing project in the nation, Burge and Stevens, consulting architects.

1935 President Franklin D. Roosevelt came to Atlanta from his Little White House retreat at Warm Springs, Georgia, to speak to the nation from Grant Field at Georgia Tech.

1936 *Gone With the Wind*, by Atlantan Margaret Mitchell (1900–1949) published; one million copies sold by December.

William B. Hartsfield elected mayor.

1937 Margaret Mitchell received Pulitzer Prize for *Gone With the Wind*.

Rhodes Center, the first shopping center in Atlanta, built at 1490–1560 Peachtree Street, Ivey & Crook, architects.

Atlanta declared a cathedral city of the Roman Catholic Church; construction of Christ the King announced (completed in 1938), Henry Dagit & Sons of Philadelphia, architects. [36.2]

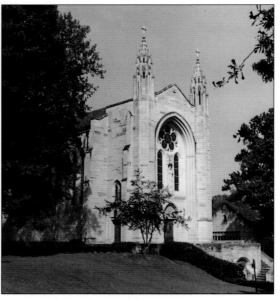

Christ the King Catholic Church, 1937. [36.2]

1939 December 15, world premier of film version of *Gone With the Wind*; the city closed down for the parade and other events surrounding the premiere. [36.3]

GWTW premiere at Loew's Grand Theatre. [36.3]

1940 Population: 302,288; greater Atlanta population: 359,000.

Hurt Park dedicated, William C. Pauley, landscape architect.

The Varsity (original building, 1940). [37.1]

The Varsity built at 61 North Avenue, Jules Gray, architect. [37.1]

Crypt of Civilization sealed (until the year 8113 A. D.) at Oglethorpe University .

1941 Pearl Harbor attacked; war with Japan declared.

Academy of Medicine built at 875 West Peachtree Street, R. Kennon Perry with Hentz, Adler & Shutze, architects. [37.2]

Academy of Medicine, 1941. [37.2]

1942 William B. Hartsfield re-elected mayor.

Whether they came from Coca-Cola or gave to it, the animations of Atlanta are like none other in these United States. People of all walks and both races live in a state of blood pressure that makes a profession of the impossible, conceive all things within their province and achieving, approach every issue in a spirit of razzle-dazzle and, without half the substance of less frenzied communities like nearby Birmingham, win on nerve, verve, and self-assertion. Long before there was a jazz age any-where else there was one in Atlanta, and long after that age has passed from hideous sight and sound its hangovers will be driving pulses on Peachtree Street.

John Temple Graves
THE FIGHTING SOUTH, 1943

1944 Ernest Woodruff, industrialist and philanthropist, died.

1945 President Franklin D. Roosevelt died at Warm Springs; the train bearing his body paused at Terminal Station as it passed through Atlanta.

Bobby Dodd named head football coach at Georgia Tech.

World War II ended.

1946 Peachtree Golf Club organized; clubhouse located in the historic Samuel House residence (c. 1857). [37.3]

Samuel House home, c. 1857. [37.3]

The Atlanta Spirit in Architecture

1946 *Song of the South*, Walt Disney's film based on Joel Chandler Harris's Uncle Remus stories, premiered in Atlanta.

One hundred nineteen people died in a fire at the Winecoff Hotel—the greatest loss of life by fire in the history of the U.S.

1947 Atlanta airport facilities greatly improved and enlarged.

The Metropolitan Opera held its first spring season at the Fox Theatre.

Metropolitan Planning Commission established.

1948 WSB-TV, the first television station in Atlanta, commenced service.

Rich's bridge over Forsyth Street, 1948. [38.1]

Rich's opened its new Store for Homes, a multi-level glass-enclosed bridge above Forsyth Street, designed by Toombs & Creighton. [38.1]

Ivan Allen, Sr., describes the Atlanta Spirit as: *Altitude and Attitude.*

1949 Margaret Mitchell died from injuries sustained when struck by a car.

Plaza Park, just south of Five Points, dedicated.

Early expressway traffic jam. [38.2]

Expressway system through the city begun. [38.2]

1950 Population: 331,314; greater Atlanta (Fulton, Dekalb, and Cobb counties) population: 664,033.

Asa Candler was always active and helpful in the creation and maintenance of what was called the "Atlanta Spirit." His own enterprise, wealth, and influence were always on call to back his almost sentimental conviction that Atlanta was destined for greatness among the cities of America . . . . He said: "The dawn of a greater Atlanta is at hand, the spirit and influence of which will spread across a horizon as yet undreamed of."
    Charles Howard Candler
    ASA GRIGGS CANDLER, 1950

1951 "Plan of Improvement" passed (to take effect January 1, 1952), expanding the city limits to annex Buckhead and Cascade Heights and other areas to the north, west, and south, increasing the city to 118 square miles in area and adding approximately 100,000 in population.

The Westminster Schools founded as an outgrowth of North Avenue Presbyterian School.

Atlanta means roughly the same as Atlantic, but she's about 200 miles from the ocean and doing all right for a mountain gal. Her patron saint is Scarlett O'Hara, and the town's just like her—shrewd, proud, and full of gumption, her Confederate slip showing under a Yankee mink coat.

James Street
HOLIDAY, 1951

1952 General Dwight D. Eisenhower came to Atlanta campaigning for the presidency.

1953 Mayor Hartsfield re-elected for his fifth term as mayor.

Washington Seminary merged with the new Westminster Schools.

Grady Hospital, 1955. [39.1]

1955 Construction of the new $24,000,000 Grady Hospital begun, along with many other important hospital projects around the city. [39.1]

The Cherokee Town and Country Club founded.

1956 Greater Atlanta had an estimated four-county population of 862,000, a one-year increase of 27,000.

Retail Credit Company (Equifax) erected headquarters at 1600 Peachtree Street, Cooper & Cooper, architects.

1957 Mayor Hartsfield won a sixth term.

Atlanta Airport became the fifth busiest airport in the nation.

Fulton National Bank built a 25-story skyscraper at Forsyth and Marietta streets, the tallest in town and the first big office building in Atlanta since the 1930s; Wyatt C. Hedrick of Dallas, Texas, and Wilner & Millkey, Atlanta, architects. [39.2]

Fulton National Bank, 1957. [39.2]

1958 Stone Mountain Memorial Park opened.

1959 Kimball House closed; built in 1885, it was razed and replaced by a parking garage.

Atlanta's spirit is varied and alert because the city is not an enlargement of any one Southern product such as cotton. Atlanta was born with energy in her body. In her genes were transportation, movement, drive.

Ralph McGill
ATLANTA JOURNAL-CONSTITUTION, October 11, 1959

Atlanta Merchandise Mart, 1961. [40.2]

Lenox Square, 1959. [40.1]

1959 Lenox Square, an open-air mall designed by Toombs, Amisano & Wells, opened on Peachtree Road just north of the Buckhead business section. (The mall is now enclosed, much altered and enlarged.) [40.1]

Masonic Temple built at 1690 Peachtree Road, Cooper & Cooper, architects.

Mayor Hartsfield described Atlanta as "a city too busy to hate."

1960 Greater Atlanta population: 1,000,000 (observed on October 10, 1959 as "M Day").

Ivan Allen, Jr., president of the Chamber of Commerce, proposed a rapid transit rail system for Atlanta.

Atlantans support plan to keep public schools open, rather than close them to oppose integration.

The Georgia Committee on Schools (Sibley Committee) recommended that Georgia repeal its laws withholding funding for integrated schools.

1961 Forward Atlanta, a national promotional campaign initiated by the Atlanta Chamber of Commerce, commenced.

Atlanta Merchandise Mart built; a 23-story skyscraper containing 1,000,000 square feet of exhibit space, it was the first important building designed and developed by architect John Portman. [40.2]

Atlanta Airport was determined to be the busiest airport in the world during certain hours; new terminal constructed.

Ivan Allen, Jr., elected mayor.

Four Atlanta high schools were integrated.

Integration begun at Georgia Tech with the acceptance of three black students.

1962 One hundred six Atlantans on a flight chartered by the Atlanta Art Association were killed in an air crash at Orly Field in Paris. The tragedy led to an expansion of the High Museum dedicated to the memory of those who perished.

Episcopal Cathedral of St. Philip dedicated at Peachtree Road in Buckhead, Francis Palmer Smith and Ivey & Crook, architects.

1963 Public parks and swimming pools and some restaurants were integrated; Mayor Ivan Allen, Jr., testifies in Washington, D. C., in support of a civil-rights act.

The Westminster Schools was the first private school to desegregate.

1964 Passage of the Civil Rights Act officially ended racial segregation.

Atlanta native Martin Luther King, Jr., civil rights leader and minister, received the Nobel Peace Prize.

Regency-Hyatt Hotel atrium, 1964. [41.1]

John Portman announced plans for a large, unique hotel for his Peachtree Center complex; featuring a twenty-one-story galleried atrium. The Regency-Hyatt House became a landmark in the use of interior commercial space; this and other construction marked a building boom of the 1960s and 1970s comparable to that of the 1920s. [41.1]

Peachtree Arcade (built in 1917) demolished to be replaced by the 41-story First National Bank tower at Five Points, Finch-Alexander-Barnes-Rothschild & Paschal, architects. [42.4]

New State Archives building constructed, A. Thomas Bradbury, architect.

1965 Mayor Ivan Allen, Jr., re-elected for second term.

Dinner held honoring Martin Luther King, Jr.; sponsored by the City of Atlanta and the Coca-Cola Company.

Atlanta Stadium, 1965. [41.2]

Atlanta Stadium, designed by two Atlanta architectural firms, Heery & Heery, with Finch, Alexander, Rothschild, Barnes, & Paschal, was completed in only fifty-one weeks. [41.2]

Lester Maddox began his rise toward political notice with his campaign against racial integration at his restaurant on Hemphill Avenue.

Peachtree Center, begun in 1965. [41.3]

Thirty-story Peachtree Center Tower built, John Portman, architect. [41.3]

1966 Song "They Are Tearin' Up Peachtree Again" published by local Lowery Music Company.

Construction begun on 103-acre Executive Park, the first major "office park" in Atlanta, at North Druid Hills Road near Interstate 85.

Atlanta Historical Society purchased the "Swan House," on Andrews Drive in Buckhead, for its headquarters.

Metropolitan Atlanta Rapid Transit Authority (MARTA) instituted.

Life of Georgia, 1966, [42.1]

C & S Tower, 1966. [42.2]

1966   Life of Georgia built a 29-story tower on a 3.1-acre landscaped site at West Peachtree and North Avenue, Bodin & Lamberson, architects. [42.1]

The Citizens and Southern National Bank built a cylinder-shaped tower designed by Richard Aeck, AIA. [42.2]

Piedmont Hotel demolished to make way for the Equitable Building, a 34-story tower on Peachtree designed by Skidmore, Owings & Merrell of New York. [42.3]

Sears opened the largest suburban department store in Atlanta and the largest Sears store in the Southeast. (An elaborate marble-faced design by Stevens & Wilkinson, it was demolished in 1985 for a high-rise office complex).

"Underground Atlanta" proposed for the center of downtown near the Zero Mile Post; developed in 1968 and 1969, it flourished in the 1970s but was closed by 1981 (redesigned by the Rouse Company, the area was reopened in 1989). [42.4]

Atlanta Civic Center built, Robert and Company, architects.

Equitable Building, 1966. [42.3]

"Underground Atlanta," 1968, and First National Bank Building, 1964. [42.4]

The hard hat has become almost as apt a symbol of Atlanta as the phoenix.
   Bruce Galphin
   ATLANTA MAGAZINE, 1967

1968   Atlanta Memorial Arts Center completed, Toombs, Amisano & Wells, architects. [42.5]

Atlanta Memorial Arts Center, 1968. [42.5]

Martin Luther King, Jr., assassinated in Memphis; funeral and burial in Dr. King's hometown of Atlanta.

New Georgia Governor's Mansion built on an 18-acre West Paces Ferry Road tract, A. Thomas Bradbury, architect.

1969 Ralph McGill, editor of the *Atlanta Constitution*, died.

Union Station demolished.

National Register of Historic Places program implemented in the state through the Georgia Historical Commission; policies now carried out through the Historic Preservation Section of the Department of Natural Resources.

Georgia State College of Business Administration became Georgia State University.

Sam Massell elected mayor; Maynard Jackson, vice-mayor.

Colony Square begun at Peachtree and Fourteenth streets, Jova/Daniels/Busby, architects. [43.1]

Atlanta is the Old South's biggest and richest city because it made itself that way. Somebody has called it "a city of optimists."
   Reg Murphy
   ATLANTA JOURNAL-CONSTITUTION, January 18, 1970

1970 Population: City, 495,144; metropolitan area, 1,458,400.

MARTA founded.

Tullie Smith House restoration begun on the grounds of the Atlanta Historical Society in conjunction with the Georgia Historical Commission.

Inman Park Restoration, Inc., organized.

First Annual Peachtree Road Race.

1971 Bulloch Hall in Roswell restored as a museum.

Old Trust Company of Georgia building, 1892, demolished for new Trust Company headquarters, Carson, Lundin, & Shaw, New York, architects. [43.2]

Colony Square, 1969. [43.1]

Trust Company of Georgia, 1971. [43.2]

1971 Edward C. Peters House on Ponce de Leon Avenue saved from demolition; Atlanta Chapter of the Victorian Society in America formed to preserve the house, which is now the Mansion restaurant.

1972 Atlanta advertised as an "international city."

1973 Lenox Square enclosed and air-conditioned.

Central City-Woodruff Park opened.

Omni, 1973, and Omni International, 1975. [44.1]

The Omni sports and convention arena opened, Thompson, Ventulett & Stainback of Atlanta, architects. [44.1]

Inman Park neighborhood recognized as a historic district on the National Register of Historic Places.

Maynard Jackson elected mayor.

In the seventies, Atlanta stands as the new American city in microcosm, still rising from the rubble of demolition and the dreams and determination of its business leaders. It is a 20th-century urban phenomenon.
Ada Louise Huxtable
NEW YORK TIMES News Service, 1974

1975 "Save the Fox" campaign succeeded; efforts coordinated by Atlanta Landmarks, Inc., a preservation organization formed to save and restore the theatre.

First MARTA station (Decatur) designed, Stevens & Wilkinson, architects.

American Institute of Architects annual convention held in Atlanta; AIA guide published.

The Omni International, a hotel-convention-office complex built at 100 Techwood Drive, Thompson, Ventulett & Stainback, architects; World Congress Center, designed by the same firm for the adjacent property, begun. [44.1]

1976 Former Georgia governor Jimmy Carter elected president of the United States.

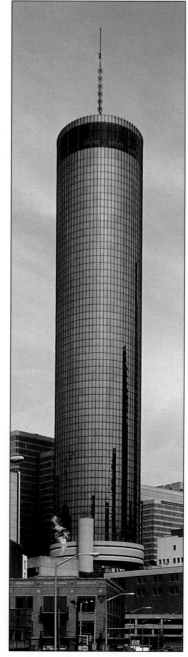

Peachtree Plaza Hotel, 1976. [44.2]

Peachtree Plaza Hotel, 70 stories tall, built on the site of the Henry Grady Hotel, John Portman, architect. [44.2]

The Coca-Cola Company erected new headquarters on North Avenue, Finch, Alexander, Barnes, Rothschild & Paschal, architects.

World Congress Center opened.

1979   Ansley Park Historic District added to the National Register of Historic Places.

New Hartsfield International Airport completed; rated the second busiest airport in the world.

1980   Population: City, 425,022; metropolitan area, 1,815,440.

Atlanta Life Insurance Company dedicated new headquarters, Joseph W. Robinson and Thompson, Ventulett, Stainback, & Associates, architects.

Atlanta Preservation Center, a city-wide organization, founded.

Southern Bell Center, 1980. [45.1]

Southern Bell Center erected on West Peachtree, Skidmore, Owings & Merrill and Finch, Alexander, Barnes, Rothschild & Paschal, architects. [45.1]

Main branch of the Atlanta-Fulton County Library moved into a new building on Carnegie Way, Marcel Breuer, architect.

1981   Andrew J. Young elected mayor.

Landmark Coca-Cola sign at Margaret Mitchell Square taken down.

1982   Georgia-Pacific headquarters erected on Peachtree at Houston, Skidmore, Owings & Merrill, architects. [45.2]

Georgia-Pacific Building, 1982. [45.2]

1983   Rhodes Hall, 1516 Peachtree Street, became headquarters of the Georgia Trust for Historic Preservation.

IBM , 1985, and A T & T, 1987, towers. [46.1]

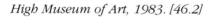

High Museum of Art, 1983. [46.2]

New High Museum of Art, designed by architect Richard Meier of New York, opened adjacent to earlier facility in the Atlanta Memorial Arts Center. [46.2]

1984   Shrine of the Immaculate Conception restored after major fire in 1982, Henry Howard Smith, architect.

"Wren's Nest" restoration announced.

1985   Hurt Building renovated.

Restoration of Healy Building begun; completed in 1987.

1985   Construction begun on IBM Tower, West Peachtree and Fourteenth streets, John Burgee and Philip Johnson of New York, architects; building opened in 1987. [46.1]

1986   The 50th anniversary of the publication of *Gone With the Wind* celebrated.

Two midtown landmarks, the Pershing Point Hotel and the Peachtree Terrace Apartments, were demolished.

Mayor Young referred to the "Castle," another midtown landmark, as a "hunk of junk."

1987   Twelve-acre, $500,000,000 office-hotel-retail development by A T & T announced, Thompson, Ventulett & Stainback, architects. Preservation of the "Castle" included in the plan. [46.1]

Conventioneers to this city, in my experience, are reporting that Atlanta itself is characterless and without charm, dull and excessively devoted to business and finance.
Arthur Frommer
Atlanta Journal-Constitution,
January 18, 1987

1988   The Democratic National Convention held in the Omni.

Greater Atlanta has come to bestride the region through . . . the sheer force of boosterism. If New York is the Big Apple and New Orleans the Big Easy, Atlanta is the Big Hustle.
John Helyar
The Wall Street Journal,
February 29, 1988

For the third straight year a Harris poll of executives rated Atlanta the best place in the United States to locate a business.

Historic Preservation Steering Committee was created to formulate a historic preservation plan for Atlanta; later an ordinance passed listing 109 recommended historic sites and 49 landmark properties.

Plans announced for Baltimore Block to be preserved as part of a larger development.

191 Tower, 1989. [47.1]

"Atlanta Spirit." . . . The term embraces a number of the finest human qualities: concern for people— vision—hard work—generosity.
Philip H. Alston, Jr.
Gardenhouse Dedication,
Atlanta Botanical Garden, 1988

1989   Construction begun on a 50-story office tower at 191 Peachtree, John Burgee and Philip Johnson, architects. [47.1]

Atlanta is a boomtown that has gone on booming; the not very old "old" Atlanta has yielded to a new and amorphous megAtlanta, with a downtown center that is for the most part . . . inanimate.
Brendan Gill
The New Yorker, January 9, 1989

The Atlanta Spirit in Architecture

One Peachtree Center Tower, 1992. [48.2]

1989 Ground broken for One Peachtree Center Tower, architect-developer John Portman's 60-story addition to his Peachtree Center Complex. [48.2]

Georgia Dome, 1992. [48.3]

It's very hard to walk around downtown Atlanta now. The tearing down and rebuilding must have been an Atlanta trademark since the first returning householder after Sherman's big fire found a few boards and nailed them together. But I think the process has been stepped up . . . . No use to ask for whom the bulldozer growls, I muttered, paraphrasing John Donne. If you live in Atlanta, it growls for thee.
Celestine Sibley
ATLANTA JOURNAL-CONSTITUTION,
November 20, 1989

The Georgia Dome, a 70,500-seat, domed sports arena, given final governmental approval. Heery International of Atlanta, primary architects, in association with Allain and Associates, Williams-Russell and Johnson, Weidlinger Associates, and Harrington and Assoiciates. Completion expected in 1992. [48.3]

I can feel this Atlanta spirit.
President George Bush
ATLANTA JOURNAL-CONSTITUTION,
October 4, 1990

Modern Atlanta dwarfs the old city center and spreads north along Peachtree Ridge with satellite skylines rising at the North Avenue and Fourteenth Street junctions. In this electronically enhanced view, John Portman's One Peachtree Center Tower and the C & S Plaza appear as finished buildings. [48.1]

Citizens and Southern National Bank announced plans for C & S Plaza, a new $200,000,000, 53-story headquarters to be completed in 1992, Kevin Roche, John Dinkeloo & Associates of New York, architects. [49.1]

Many who move to Atlanta for their jobs fall in love with the city. Maybe its the quality of life, that mixture of old-time Southern gentility with the energy of modern growing Atlanta.
ATLANTA JOURNAL-CONSTITUTION,
February 5, 1989

1990   Population: Metropolitan area, 2,833,511, twelfth largest in the nation.

Population Crisis Committee study ranked Atlanta fourth among world cities for the most favorable urban living standards.

Gullstedt Gruppen, a Swedish company, announced construction plans for a 50-story mixed-use GLG Tower on Fourteenth Street.

September 19, Atlanta named host city for the Games of the XXVIth Olympiad, to be held in the summer of 1996, the centennial of the modern Olympic Games.

C & S Plaza, 1992. [49.1]

Winning the Olympics is the latest example of our vision, our faith, and our cooperation. Clearly, we don't just let things happen—we make them happen. Therefore, we cannot just let the face of our city change—we must direct the energy of these events and make it happen in the best manner possible.

John Portman
ATLANTA JOURNAL-CONSTITUTION,
May 12, 1991

Landmarks of Atlanta Residential Architecture

The best suburbs of Atlanta are first rate . . . almost unequalled for the quality of their neighborhood planning and the extreme excellence of their houses and gardens.

H. Stafford Bryant, Jr.
CLASSICAL AMERICA 1990

IN 1926 THE GROWING City of Atlanta, not yet one hundred years old, officially divided itself into four sectors: N.W., N.E., S.W., and S.E., centered in downtown Atlanta at Edgewood Avenue and Pryor Street, where Woodruff Park is today. This intersection, one block east of Peachtree Street at Five Points, is 1,046 feet above sea level, only blocks from the highest point within the city limits—Capitol Square, at 1,050 feet. It is also a few blocks from the Zero Mile Post, the historic center of the old town; this post marked the terminus of the Western and Atlantic Railroad. This optimum location had been determined by engineers' land surveys, and the original settlement, first called Terminus and later changed to Marthasville, began to grow around that spot, six miles east of the Chattahoochee River on the prominent ridge extending from the southwest to the northeast. Peachtree Ridge, with an average elevation of 1,000 feet, became the central spine of the city.

When the town of Marthasville became the City of Atlanta in 1847, the first city limits were drawn in a one-mile radius from the Zero Mile Post; and the city began to spread for miles around. From where the railroads crossed in the vicinity of modern Five Points, and from the pivotal point of the city's four sectors in that same area, metropolitan Atlanta had spread over eighteen counties by the 150th anniversary of Terminus in 1987.

The earliest neighborhoods were clustered around Five Points, where

Cherokee is among the many beautiful roads which contribute to Buckhead's reputation as one of the finest residential areas in the nation.

Peachtree, Marietta, Decatur, and Edgewood meet, but this junction soon became the busy center of commerce, which, aided by the new convenience of mule-drawn streetcars, began to push residential settlements out in all directions, eventually far outside the original radius. The first streetcar line went south in 1871 toward the village of West End, which became an early elite suburb, the home of many notable citizens, including Evan P. Howell, publisher of the *Atlanta Constitution*. The next went north out Peachtree Street, fast becoming the city's most fashionable thoroughfare, lined with trees, ornate fences, fine two-story residences, and tall church spires. The state governor's mansion and the Leyden house were two of the most notable dwellings in Peachtree's brief but significant residential heyday.

Even though the commercial district was spreading rapidly, the old Maxwell R. Berry home had stood within walking distance of the central business district, at the corner of Walton and Fairlie Streets as late as 1909. As the Berry place was being torn down, the *Atlanta Journal* reported, November 14, 1909: "One more landmark of Atlanta's village day is going. . . . All is going—every last shred of brick, every last crumb of old mortar. . . . For the city has outgrown them. They are downtown where they don't belong." (This attitude, an old one in Atlanta,

may be changing in the 1990s.)

Typically in piedmont towns located near rivers, the commercial center is on the plain by the river, and the more exclusive neighborhoods eventually develop in the higher elevations of the surrounding hills. The commerce of Atlanta, however, was tied to the railroads, not the Chattahoochee, and the commercial center developed around the highest ridge. The old Berry house near Five Points was on land higher in elevation than the newly developing

Top: An 1864 view from Ellis Street toward "College Hill," now Clifford Street. Above: An early "Terminus" building, supposedly the first two-story structure in the town, was moved several times before being torn down around 1917. Below left: The home of architect John Boutell, built at the southwest corner of Ellis and Collins (now Courtland) streets, was demolished in 1938. Below right: The John Neal house, designed by Boutell and built in 1859 on Washington Street at Mitchell, was torn down in 1929.

had been sited atop the highest hill on the ridge, and the greatest building activity grew along its course. A natural path followed the top of this 1,000-foot-high ridge, and the thoroughfare that developed with the young town became synonymous with Atlanta. Peachtree Street began as an Indian trail, but by the 1880s and 1890s it had become one of the most prestigious residential addresses in the South, extending from Ellis Street just north of Five Points, out to the Tenth Street area, and later as far as Buckhead and beyond.

Peachtree Ridge was a geographically strategic location, the gateway to the west from the Atlantic seaboard states. West of the ridge the Chattahoochee River flows to the Gulf of Mexico, and on the east the South River and the several large creeks drain into a river system which ends in the Atlantic Ocean. The ridge was also the historic dividing line between the Creek and Cherokee nations.

Peachtree Ridge is in the upper section of the Piedmont Plateau, the "foot of the mountains," characterized by elevations of 600 to 1,200 feet, a rolling terrain covered with hardwoods and pine trees. Indeed, some historians have speculated that Peachtree may have instead originally been "pitch tree," for a tall pine that grew near the river crossing. The earliest records of white settlers such as Hardy Ivy, Hardy

posh residential neighborhoods of north Atlanta: Ansley Park is 900-950 feet; Druid Hills, 900-1,000; and Peachtree Heights Park, 900-1,000. In only a few years the hills of northwest Atlanta in the Buckhead district would attract the prosperous descendants of early settlers such as Maxwell Berry, but their homes would be on ground no more elevated than his farm-like homeplace had been at Five Points.

At first the city hall, and then the state capitol, rightly and symbolically,

Above: The serenity of Ansley Park, typified by the Neel Reid designed Black-Clarke house, belies the proximity of the bustling Midtown commercial district. Below left: Along winding Habersham Road are found some of the most distinguished homes in Buckhead. Below right: Lullwater Road meanders along Lullwater Creek through rolling, tree-shaded Druid Hills.

Residential Architecture

Right: Peachtree Street between Ellis and Cain streets in 1890. From left are the old Capital City Club (originally the second John H. James mansion, 1885, demolished in 1912), the Richards-Abbott house (1884), and the Austin Leyden house (c. 1859, designed by John Boutell, demolished in 1913). This was the block of Peachtree where Scarlett O'Hara Butler built her dream house in Gone With the Wind. *On this site today, the Capital City Club has been replaced by Macy's, the rest of the block is the location of the Westin Peachtree Plaza Hotel, which rises seventy stories.*

Austin Leyden house (c. 1859).

Governor's Mansion, originally the first John H. James mansion (1869).

Samuel M. Inman house (1890).

Pace, and George W. Collier, however, usually referred to the Creek Indian settlement at the confluence of the Chattahoochee River and Peachtree Creek as Standing Peachtree.

Although "Peachtree," in fact and legend, is so strongly identified with the city, "Piedmont" is probably the second most familiar name to long-time Atlantans: Piedmont Avenue and Road, Piedmont Park, Piedmont Hospital, and Piedmont Driving Club, to name some of the best known, all point to the city's location in the midst of piedmont topography. These rolling hills provided beautiful areas for suburban developments, a mosaic of neighborhoods in all four sectors of the city, with

Peachtree and Piedmont as central spines around which many of the most lasting and best-known neighborhoods have been developed.

Undoubtedly the railroad surveyors and engineers found a beautiful terrain within the wooded land lots near the Chattahoochee River. Dr. George Gilman Smith, a Methodist minister and historian who had lived in Atlanta from 1847 until 1855, reminisced in a newspaper memoir published in 1909: "I have seen few things as fair as were the Atlanta woods in 1848." Smith added (but we can no longer say): "When a stream was found, it was as clear as crystal." A Boston journalist, Sidney Andrews, who passed through

Except for the Georgia Capitol, little remains of the affluent Capitol View neighborhood, where splendid homes such as the two below once stood.

T. P. Westmoreland house (1893).

Below, both pages: As Peachtree Street followed the natural contours of the ridge north from Five Points, its elevation remained at about 1,000 feet, and it consequently afforded desirable building sites. Until the early years of the twentieth century some of Atlanta's most notable citizens lived along its most famous street. Among them were the James, Leyden, Block, Grant, Inman, and Mitchell families, whose Peachtree homes are pictured below. The Mitchell house was the girlhood home of novelist Margaret Mitchell, who, like Scarlett, valued her Peachtree address.

John W. Grant house (1890).

Frank E. Block house (1892).

Eugene M. Mitchell house (1911).

The omniverous appetite for new buildings in downtown Atlanta usually meant a short life for houses, but the Brown home lasted until 1957.

Julius Brown house (1885).

in December 1865, about a year after General Sherman had burned the Confederate town practically to the ground, wrote later: "From all this ruin and devastation a new city is springing up with marvelous rapidity. . . . The four railroads centered here groan with freight and passenger traffic." He continued and made a prediction, the latter part of which has come true: "It can never be a handsome city, but its surrounding hills and slopes offer beautiful sites for elegant residences."

Indeed, and Atlantans have taken advantage of this natural setting to create through the years some of the most beautiful neighborhoods in America. Only recently H. Stafford Bryant, Jr.,

wrote for *Classical America*: "The best suburbs of Atlanta are first rate . . . almost unequalled for the quality of their neighborhood planning and the extreme excellence of their houses and gardens."

Atlanta's long reputation as a city of beautiful homes and gentle hospitality derives largely from its leafy, residential suburbs. The following gazetteer describes a number of planned Atlanta neighborhoods; thankfully, many are being preserved as living parts of viable communities through the help of vigilant civic associations. Succeeding the gazetteer is a choice selection from these neighborhoods of landmark homes which are truly "classic" Atlanta.

Neighborhoods Gazetteer

West End: Evan P. Howell house (c. 1885).

Scene in Grant Park around the turn of the century.

East Lake Country Club (1905–06).

West End. This area southwest of downtown Atlanta grew from White Hall Tavern, which stood near the present crossing of Lee and Gordon streets in 1835. It was incorporated in 1868. A street car line in 1871–72 brought further growth to West End, and in 1894 it was annexed to Atlanta. Built according to a formal grid pattern centering on Gordon Street, West End has been called the city's first "upper-class suburb." Captain Evan P. Howell (C.S.A.), a West End resident, owned the *Atlanta Constitution*, and on April 27, 1890, the paper noted: "West End is emphatically a residence community of a thrifty, well-to-do class of people, who generally own their homes, who have their gardens, their flower yard, their horse, cow, and fowls, and, away from the noise and dust of the great city, live in quiet and comfort." Howell Park and Joel Chandler Harris's Wren's Nest are landmarks left from its elite period in the 1880s and 1890s. In the vicinity of these two landmarks the neighborhood is undergoing a residential renascence. Elevation 1,000 feet.

Grant Park. In 1883 Colonel L. P. Grant deeded 85 acres of his farm to the city as a park; around this park, later enlarged and named for him, a middle-class neighborhood grew up. A line of the Atlanta Street Railway Company, terminating at Oakland Cemetery, served the area, and later Colonel Grant built a car line to his neighborhood, where he had lived since the 1850s. His second home there, a stuccoed Italianate villa on Hill Street, survives as one of the landmarks of the revitalized neighborhood. Built on a grid pattern around Grant Park, the neighborhood lies at 900 to 1,025 feet elevation. On the hills south of the capitol, Grant Park is all that remains of the once extensive residential developments, most of which were torn down along Washington Street and Capitol and Georgia avenues to build Atlanta Stadium and Interstate 20. The Grant Park Neighborhood Association, formed in the 1970s, sponsors an annual fall tour of homes and festival and has listed the area as a district on the National Register of Historic Places (NR).

East Lake. Due east of Grant Park, out Memorial Drive in Dekalb County, East Lake was an antebellum suburban resort and settlement. A landmark of that era is the Robert A. Alston house, "Meadowbrook" (1856), at 2420 Alston Drive. In 1908 East Lake was incorporated as a town around the East Lake Country Club, Atlanta's first country club. Built by the Atlanta Athletic Club in 1905–06, the East Lake golf club was Bobby Jones's home course; he won his first junior championship here in 1911 when he was nine. The town was annexed to Atlanta in 1928. Elevation 1,000 feet.

Peters Park. In 1884 Richard Peters, H. I. Kimball, and others planned a subdivision on part of Peters's land in the area—now called Midtown—along either side of Peachtree Street south of Eighth Street and north of North Avenue. Little of the formal aspects of the plan was built, but Kimball and Peters both built their homes in the neighborhood, on Peachtree in the vicinity of where the Fox Theater was built in 1929. As late as 1954 the Peters Land Company was still in

business and had land remaining for sale from the 202.5-acre Land Lot 49 that Richard Peters purchased in 1849. Peters Park and the Peachtree Street car line that Peters built were two of the reasons people began to move north away from Five Points in the 1880s and 1890s. Richard's son, Edward C. Peters, built a home on three and one-half acres at Ponce de Leon and Piedmont avenues, and it still stands preserved as part of a restaurant called "The Mansion." It is one of the last landmarks of Peters Park. The oldest section of the Georgia Institute of Technology campus is on land originally part of Peters Park.

Old Fourth Ward District. This neighborhood, adjacent to the "Sweet Auburn" business district, was the home of many of Atlanta's most prominent black leaders. Among those who called this area home were: Bishop William A. Fountain; Antoine Graves; David Tobias Howard; John Wesley Dobbs; and Ossiam Flipper, the first black cadet to graduate from the United States Military Academy at West Point.

Inman Park. In 1889 Joel Hurt, a civil engineer-businessman influenced by Frederick Law Olmsted, began this planned suburb as part of an overall scheme that included an electric street railway and a skyscraper located downtown, a mile west on Edgewood and Pryor. Presently being restored, the neighborhood has many landmark houses and other structures and features, including Springvale Park and live oak trees planted by Joel Hurt. The Beath-Dickey-Griggs house at 866 Euclid Avenue, one of the first and finest in the neighborhood, has been restored as a private home and has been an inspiration to other restorationists throughout the city. Inman Park is a historic district on the National Register of Historic Places. Just west of Decatur, Inman Park is at 1,000 feet elevation.

Peters Park. Above: Edward C. Peters house (1885).

Inman Park. Above: Houses on Edgewood Avenue (c. 1890). Below: Callan Castle (1889).

Druid Hills. Above: Emory University Campus.
Below: Asa Candler home on Ponce de Leon Avenue.

Buckhead. Above: Andrews Drive.
Below: Habersham Road.

Druid Hills. Joel Hurt obtained the original plan for Druid Hills in 1893 from Frederick Law Olmsted; the final plan dates from 1905, prepared by Olmsted Brothers. Druid Hills was not opened for development until 1908, when Asa G. Candler, the Coca-Cola magnate, purchased the project. Ponce de Leon Avenue was the main thoroughfare. Many landmarks survive, including several Candler mansions and the Emory University campus, a Henry Hornbostel design. Many fine houses stand exactly as designed by talented architects, such as Neel Reid and Lewis Edmund Crook, a Reid protégé. The Druid Hills Golf Club on Ponce de Leon at Clifton Road, dating from 1912, still operates and is a major landmark. Lullwater Road, one of Atlanta's most beautiful residential streets, overlooks the golf course and Lullwater Creek, as it winds its way between Ponce de Leon and North Decatur Road toward the Emory campus. (The film *Driving Miss Daisy* featured a Lullwater Road mansion.) Much of Druid Hills is on the National Register. Elevation 900–1,000 feet.

Oakland City-Sylvan Hills. Incorporated in 1894, Oakland City was developed along a grid pattern south of West End, and west of Lee Street. The elevation is only a few feet lower than that at Capitol Square. An active neighborhood association sponsors tours of the neighborhood as restoration proceeds. Sylvan Hills, originally a small streetcar subdivision of Oakland City, grew in conjunction with adjacent Fort McPherson, the United States military reservation, which was developed at about the same time.

Candler Park-Edgewood. A National Register district just east of Inman Park and adjacent to Kirkwood, this neighborhood surrounds Candler Park, one of the city's oldest community parks (1922). Edgewood, originally a railroad stop, was incorporated in 1899 but was annexed to Atlanta in 1909. The Smith-Benning house, 520 Oakdale Road, is a landmark of early Edgewood.

Kirkwood. Developed east of Inman Park in 1899, Kirkwood adjoins Decatur along the railroad track. Many of its landmarks have been lost, but some of its houses have been restored. Kirkwood was annexed to Atlanta in 1922. Elevation 1,050.

Buckhead. In 1838 Henry Irby of South Carolina erected a tavern-grocery store at the intersection of Peachtree, Roswell, and Paces Ferry roads, elevation 1,000 feet, which became a gathering place within the Buckhead voting district. This intersection is the longtime center of the present-day Buckhead community, the most well-to-do and elegant residential area within the city limits. (Buckhead was brought into the city in 1952 under the Plan of Improvement.) Buckhead has many planned neighborhoods of the garden suburb type, among them Garden Hills, Peachtree Heights Park, Haynes Manor, and Tuxedo Park, all developed in the first decades of the twentieth century and some of which are on the National Register of Historic Places. West Paces Ferry Road is still the site of many beautiful estates, including the Georgia Governor's Mansion. On Andrews Drive nearby is the Edward Inman estate, Swan House, today the headquarters of the Atlanta Historical Society. Swan House was designed for the Inmans in 1926 by Philip Trammell Shutze, FAIA, of the noted Atlanta architectural firm of Hentz, Reid & Adler.

Ansley Park. In 1904–05 Edwin P. Ansley began a development on farm land that had belonged to the Collier family, original Atlanta settlers. His civil engineer was Solon Z. Ruff, engineer for Druid Hills and a disciple of Frederick Law Olmsted. Ansley Park, at first called Peachtree Garden, was Atlanta's first truly successful garden suburb and is still one of the most desirable neighborhoods. As part of the original layout, Ansley planned a golf course and polo field, now the private Ansley Golf Club, founded in 1912. Ansley Park and Piedmont Park were laid out in tandem to compliment each other; their entrance roadways, for example, match, and the two were often called "Twin Parks." Within the suburb many park-like areas were planned, such as Winn Park. The streets curve and follow the piedmont topography. The Peachtree Street side of the neighborhood has landmarks such as the First Church of Christ, Scientist at Fifteenth Street and just north, The Reid House. On the Piedmont Avenue side is the Piedmont Driving Club. Begun in a farmhouse in 1887 as the

Ansley Park. Above: An 1895 view of the Piedmont Driving Club, begun in the old Walker farmhouse. Below: Peachtree Circle, about 1910.

Gentlemen's Driving Club, it is now much enlarged and enhanced with elegant additions. The elevation of Ansley Park varies from 900 to 950 feet. It is on the National Register of Historic Places as "Atlanta's first automobile suburb." (Ansley Park is now part of Midtown, a designation coined in 1972 for the area roughly between North Avenue and Pershing Point, Monroe Drive and Georgia Tech.) The old Tenth Street shopping district along Peachtree Street between Tenth and Fourteenth streets, an area once called Tight Squeeze, which traditionally served Ansley Park and much of Midtown, has almost disappeared with the construction of high-rise buildings, a pattern which began in the 1960s with the creation of the Colony Square complex at Peachtree and Fourteenth streets.

Atkins Park. This subdivision, developed in 1910 by Edwin Grove on the western edge of Druid Hills just off Ponce de Leon Avenue, consists of three parallel streets, St. Louis, St. Charles, and St. Augustine places, and is entered at either side of the subdivision through rock piers on North Highland Avenue and Briarcliff Road. Elevation 990 feet; on the National Register of Historic Places.

Ansley Park. Below: The Reid House (1923).

Brookhaven. Above: A 1915 view of clubhouse.

Peachtree Heights Park. Above: View of entrance at Peachtree Road and Peachtree Battle Avenue, about 1915. Below: Habersham and Rivers roads.

Tuxedo Park. Right: Joseph D. Rhodes house (1926), West Paces Ferry Road.

Brookhaven. The Capital City Country Club is called Brookhaven. This neighborhood, begun in 1910, was the first in Atlanta planned around a golf course, and was called Atlanta's "first country club community." Club Drive is a major thoroughfare through the area, which lies west of Peachtree in Dekalb County; elevation 900–960 feet. (NR)

Peachtree Heights Park. Eretus Rivers, for whom the E. Rivers Grammar School at the entrance to the area was named, developed this elegant neighborhood with Walter P. Andrews beginning in 1911 west of Peachtree Road and south of the Buckhead shopping area. The noted New York architectural firm of Carrere & Hastings designed the street layout, with median-park enhanced Peachtree Battle Avenue and curving Habersham Road as significant streets. The neighborhood is like one great landscaped park dotted with well-designed "period" houses. This is undoubtedly the quintessence of Atlanta's garden suburb style, much-admired for well over a half-century. Anne Rivers Siddons, in her novel *Peachtree Road* (Harper & Row, 1988), described this part of Atlanta: "Residential Buckhead, that cloistered, deep green rectangle of great old trees and winding streets and fine, not-so-old houses set far back on emerald green lawns, carved out of deep hardwood forests, cushioned and insulated from the . . . cacophony of the city proper, to the south, by layers of money. No one has ever been quite sure what the official boundaries of Buckhead are but for many years my own personal Buckhead was that four square miles bounded on the south by Peachtree Creek, the north by West Paces Ferry Road, the west by Northside Drive, and the east by Peachtree Road." Elevation 900–1,000 feet. (NR)

Peachtree Heights East. Platted in 1910 and developed east of Peachtree Road along with Peachtree Heights Park, which was on the west side of Peachtree. Lots in Peachtree Heights East were smaller and houses less costly, many not designed by architects, but the amenities included a small lake and much wooded open space. East Wesley Road is a major road through to Piedmont Road. Because of its convenience and relatively more modest cost, this is one of Atlanta's most sought-after residential areas. Elevation 850–950 feet.

Tuxedo Park. Charles H. Black developed this elegant area from 1911 through the 1920s and 1930s, building houses practically all designed by leading architects, among them the Atlanta firm of Frazier & Bodin. Some of the places would qualify as estates. Coca-Cola magnate Robert W. Woodruff lived on Tuxedo Road. This is the Druid Hills of northwest Atlanta, very much in the tradition of Frederick Law Olmsted's planned naturalistic landscapes. Valley Road follows the

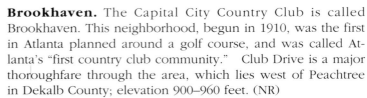

course of Wolf Creek through the area, creating the illusion of a north Georgia mountain retreat; elevation 800–1,000 feet.

Peachtree Hills. East of Peachtree Road from Peachtree Creek north to Lindbergh Drive and east toward Piedmont Avenue, Peachtree Hills was developed on the thirteen-hundred-acre farm of pioneer settler Benjamin Plaster. Originally called Peachtree Hills Place, the first lots were sold in 1912 for five hundred dollars each. One of the major landmarks of the neighborhood is the 315-unit Peachtree Hills apartment complex, an early award-winning example of International Style modernism, designed by Stevens & Wilkerson and built in 1938 by the J. A. Jones Construction Company. With all of Buckhead, the area was annexed to Atlanta in 1952. The Peachtree Hills Civic Association emphasizes the diversity and neighborhood spirit of a place in which residents still walk to convenient nearby churches and stores.

Garden Hills. Annexed to Atlanta as part of the Buckhead area in 1952, Garden Hills was begun in 1925 by P. C. Mc-Duffie, an Atlanta attorney. It stretches from Peachtree Road east to Piedmont Road. In 1931 North Fulton High School, designed by the firm of Hentz, Adler & Shutze, was added to the development. A clubhouse and swimming pool in the center of the subdivision are now a city park. Rumson Road is a central spine of this garden suburb just north of Peachtree Heights East. Elevation 850–950 feet. (NR)

Brookwood Hills. South of Garden Hills and north of Ansley Park is this well-defined residential area with limited access from Peachtree Road at Huntington, Palisades, and Brighton roads. Developers Benjamin Franklin Burdett and Arthur Clinton Burdett bought fifty acres from the A. J. Collier estate in 1912 to begin the first phase of the neighborhood; by 1922 there were sixty-five acres. The civil engineer who planned the naturalistic layout was O. F. Kaufman. Part of the original plan was a community pool and recreation area, named for the Burdettes in 1974, and now a private club. Brookwood Hills was designed for upper-middle-class automobile owners and is still considered one of Atlanta's most desirable garden suburbs. It is convenient and beautiful, with elegant, traditional two-story single-family residences, most dating from the 1920s and 1930s. Many were designed by leading names in the history of Atlanta's domestic architecture. The active neighborhood civic association sponsored the addition of Brookwood Hills to the National Register of Historic Places in 1979. Elevation 900 feet.

Haynes Manor. Dating from the late 1920s, it was built as an extension of Peachtree Heights Park toward Northside Drive. Peachtree Creek flows through a portion of Haynes Manor, and the Bobby Jones Golf Course, a city park, defines its southern boundary. Elevation 850 feet.

Collier Hills. H. W. Nicholes and Sons, leading Atlanta house contractors, developed this garden suburb in the 1930s and 1940s south of the Bobby Jones Golf Course along Collier Road on the hills above Tanyard Creek. The land had belonged to the Andrew Jackson Collier estate and was the site of some of the hardest fighting in the Battle of Peachtree Creek in the summer of 1864. The Nicholeses built this community of stylish cottages, largely in the Colonial Revival mode, amidst wooded parks. It is convenient to Peachtree Road businesses and churches and to Northside Drive, a main north-south thoroughfare. Elevation 850-900 feet.

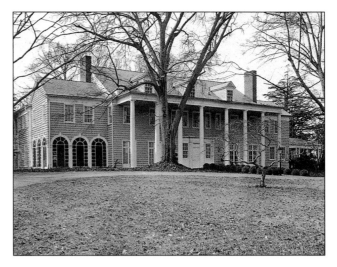

Tuxedo Park. Above: James L. Dickey house (1914–17). Below: John W. Grant, Sr., house, now the Cherokee Country Club.

Tuxedo Park. Below: Robert F. Maddox house, "Woodhaven" (1911), now the site of the Georgia Governor's Mansion on West Paces Ferry Road.

Atlanta University Center. Above: Clark College, Chrisman Hall (1877).

Northeast Lot-Atlanta University Center. Above: Alonzo Herndon house (1910).

Atlanta University Center. Below: Spelman College, Rockefeller Hall (1885).

Northeast Lot-Atlanta University Center. About 1910 this small enclave of fine black-owned residences was begun adjacent to Atlanta University; included is the neoclassical mansion of Alonzo Herndon, founder of Atlanta Life Insurance Company. The Herndon home is now a house museum. The Atlanta University Center is, like much of downtown Atlanta, around 1,000 feet elevation. Atlanta's "West Side" has long been a center of black life and culture, rivaling that centered on Auburn Avenue.

Vine City. Just north of the Atlanta University Center, near the site of the Georgia Dome, is the diverse and interesting neighborhood of Vine City. Settled primarily by blacks who came to the "West Side" after being displaced by the great 1917 fire, Vine City houses reflect a heterogeneous residential mix of the affluent, middle-class, and poor..

West Side Park. Just west of Atlanta University and Morris Brown College, the black-owned Service Realty Company developed this subdivision of bungalows for middle-class blacks in 1924. Within the immediate area are Washington Park and Booker T. Washington High School, landmarks on the "West Side." Elevation 950 feet.

Washington Park. Prior to World War I, this neighborhood was white, but between 1922 and 1928, it became the focus of a growing effort by middle-class blacks for autonomy. Led by developer and entrepreneur Herman Perry, activists acquired Washington Park, Atlanta's first black park. The area was also the location of the city's first black subdivision.

Collier Heights. In the late 1930s, black Atlantans began the development of Collier Heights west of Atlanta University on wooded, rolling terrain. Many of the houses date from the 1950s and 1960s, and today the area is home to some of the city's most successful and influential citizens, one of whom, State Representative J. E. McKinney, has said: "Collier Heights was built by blacks, for blacks, on land owned by blacks." The two-square-mile area, with an estimated seven thousand residents, has a vital civic association which has sponsored such neighborhood amenities as Harwell Heights Park and Frederick Douglass High School.

Cascade Heights-Audubon Forest. Southwest of West End out Cascade Road near historic Cascade Springs and along Sandtown and Sewell Roads, these adjacent neighborhoods were laid out in the years between 1925 and 1955, with curving streets around the Adams Park Golf Course, a city park in Cascade Heights, the older of the two subdivisions; Audubon Forest was developed just after World War II. A landmark house in the area is the old Thomas Pitts place at 3105 Cascade Road, an unusually large bungalow designed by Leila

Ross Wilburn for the ten-acre dairy farm. Elevation 900–1,000 feet.

Virginia-Highland-North Boulevard Park-Orme Park. On the east side of Piedmont Park this community of bungalows and cottages was developed before and after the First World War. East of "Midtown," Monroe Drive and Park Drive are centers of the general neighborhood, as is the commercial crossroads at Virginia and Highland avenues, elevation 980 feet at the intersection. The Samuel Inman Elementary School at Park Drive and Virginia Avenue, built in 1923, is an operating landmark, as is Grady High School, built in 1932 on Monroe Drive at Charles Allen Drive and Tenth Street. Active neighborhood associations sponsor house and garden tours and lobby to represent the interests of this old intown suburban community adjacent to "Midtown."

Morningside Park. Developed by James R. Smith and M. S. Rankin in the 1920s and 1930s east of Piedmont Avenue with Rock Springs Road as a major thoroughfare, Morningside, like many older Atlanta neighborhoods, is having a revival. Popular again is the prevailing style of architecture, a simplified Tudor Revival brick cottage with gables and suggestions of half timbering. Morningside was annexed by Atlanta in 1925. Elevation 900 feet.

Lenox Park. Herbert Kaiser, a developer, and the architects Ivey & Crook planned this eastern addition to Morningside in 1931, according to the garden suburb mold, with forested parks. Ivey & Crook designed model houses in period architectural style: two of them, "The Barclay" and "The Sussex," were built and are still lived in. The Morningside-Lenox Park Association, which successfully blocked the building of I-485 through the area, has erected classical piers, replicating those Ivey & Crook designed for Lenox Park, to mark entrances into the entire neighborhood.

Peachtree Highlands. East of Piedmont Avenue in the Buckhead area, this neighborhood was designed for the middle class in the early 1920s. Elevation 900-950 feet. It is on the National Register of Historic Places and has an active neighborhood association.

Avondale Estates. Beginning in the mid 1920s, George F. Willis, an Atlanta patent medicine tycoon, developed this English Tudor style village as an incorporated town of one thousand acres, just east of Decatur. In Dekalb County, but always considered an Atlanta suburb, Avondale Estates features a Tudor style commercial center and a planned district of one hundred houses, with a lake, parkways, and other landscaped areas. The historic core of the city was listed on the National Register of Historic Places in 1986. Elevation 900 feet.

Morningside-Lenox Park. Above: Replica of Ivey & Crook designed classical piers. Below: Ivey & Crook design for model house in Lenox Park.

Avondale Estates. Below: Tudor style commercial center.

Landmark Homes
of Atlanta

Atlantans are renowned for the taste and sumptuousness of their residences in a green setting of trees, shrubbery, and sweeping hills . . . . Yet this notable architecture has developed from an origin of pioneer crudeness within a century.

ATLANTA, A CITY OF THE MODERN SOUTH, 1942

The Childs-Jones-Peterson house in Buckhead's Tuxedo Park was designed by Philip Trammell Shutze in 1928. The entrance elevation, inspired by the Barchessa Valmarano in northern Italy, overlooks a sloping green lawn where Bobby Jones, the second owner of the house, once practiced putting.

ARCHITECTURAL HISTORIAN Professor James H. Grady of Georgia Tech wrote about this house when Robert N. Griggs had completed the initial phase of its restoration, "The architect of the Griggs house is unknown but it is a good example of the rich, picturesque, infinitely varied English Aesthetic Movement. Interiors are richly detailed and have been carefully restored." ("A Question of Style, Houses in Atlanta, 1885–1900," *Yale Perspecta*, 1975).

Queen Anne is the name of the Victorian style often given to the American phase of the Aesthetic Movement. Robert Griggs's Queen Anne villa is a landmark in the preservation and restoration of Victorian architecture in

Atlanta, in the rehabilitation of an entire Victorian-period neighborhood, and a landmark of private restoration in Atlanta of the kind that now occurs more frequently, encouraged by such examples as that of the Beath-Griggs house.

In some ways, this house is more significant as a restoration than it was as an Inman Park residence of the 1890s, although it was one of the best

Above: Entrance elevation on Euclid Avenue. Left: Garden elevation. Opposite above: Living hall and front stairs. Right: Living hall looking into rear stair hall and dining room.

houses built in the neighborhood. As Inman Park's most important restoration, it has attained historical status. In July 1973 the entire Inman Park neighborhood—as originally planned and developed—was recognized as a historic district and added to the National Register of Historic Places. The Beath–Griggs house was singled out for its preeminent place in the renovation of the community.

Atlanta's first planned suburb, Inman Park (1888) was the brainchild of Joel Hurt (1850–1926), a civil engineer and entrepreneur who was one of the most influential figures in creating the spirit of New South in Atlanta. Hurt bought a large acreage several miles

east of the newly built State Capitol. Using a layout similar to that of the picturesque garden suburbs of Llewellyn Park in New Jersey (1860) and Riverside, near Chicago (1868), he landscaped the existing terrain, with native trees and shrubs, adding curving streets, fair-sized building lots, a park, a lake, and exotic plant materials such as coastal Georgia live oak trees.

Hurt's planned suburban setting for the display of Queen Anne villas was based on the land-use and design ideas of Andrew Jackson Downing and Frederick Law Olmsted. Other comprehensively planned Atlanta neighborhoods were built soon afterwards, notably Ansley Park and Druid Hills and then in northwest Atlanta, giving other choices of fine neighborhoods for growing Atlanta to settle in. The introduction of the automobile soon detracted from the convenience of Hurt's electric street railway along Edgewood Avenue, rendering Inman Park less fashionably suburban than nearby Druid Hills, and the Queen Anne style also began to lose fashion. Atlanta's most sought-after and talented architect of suburban houses in the 1910s and 1920s, Neel Reid, designed only one Inman Park house.

But by the 1960s the trend had begun to slowly reverse as the growing problems of the community coincided with a change in architectural taste and an interest in inner-city life. The old suburbs slowly became urban as the city spread farther and farther away from the capitol and Five Points. Inman Park was not the first to experience this change; there were young couples at this time who moved into Ansley Park, which, unlike Inman Park, had never been taken over by slumlords. Robert Griggs, an Atlanta native and bachelor, led the trend in the more adventurous direction of Inman Park. Perhaps only a single person would have attempted what he did in 1969.

That year Bob Griggs paid $22,500 for his three-story dream house, which many people would have considered a Charles Addams nightmare. Almost the whole of Inman Park had become a temporary stopping place for people near to being homeless. Each of the thirteen rooms of his house had become a separate apartment, housing forty people in all. Griggs, a profes-

sional designer and artist, saw the grandeur under the ugly paint and grime—a spiral staircase, carved woodwork, tarnished silver hardware on bird's-eye maple doors, and original tiled mantelpieces. The challenge of this "grimy grandeur" appealed to him, although he knew that it would be difficult ever to match the unknown de-

Opposite top: Detail of dining room overdoor carving. Left: Dining room chimney breast. Above: Drawing room with original woodwork. Right: The drawing room mantel features painted tile with James M. Beath's monogram and Georgia flora and fauna.

signer and craftsmen of 866 Euclid. He spent more than $50,000 in the early 1970s to turn it into a single-family dwelling again. Others following his lead would bring the neighborhood back to a point many doubted it would ever see again. Along the way Inman Park Restoration and an Atlanta chapter of the Victorian Society in America were formed.

Griggs shares the three-story Queen Anne house with a landscape architect, Robert B. Aiken, a native of Brunswick, Georgia, who joined the effort in the 1970s. The grounds show his professional touch, and, with two professional designers in residence, the house, inside and out, is the realization of a modern dream and a showplace that probably exceeds even the original owner's expectations.

The house was built for John M. Beath, who had come to Atlanta, made a fortune, and lavished it on this house as a honeymoon gift to his bride. The mantelpiece in the drawing room has his monogram and Atlanta's most beautiful Victorian fireplace tiles, an unequalled display of local flora and fauna in the taste of the Aesthetic Movement.

Everything about the place shows the Victorians' exuberant love of history and nature. The interior and exterior have that oddly attractive and extravagant combination that characterized the late nineteenth century: the formal and classical, the informal and the naturalistic, imaginatively and eclectically combined. Typical of the era are free-flowing interior spaces; a taut exterior skin of earth-toned shingles; a decoratively rich display of materials: granite, brick, marble, slate, wood, wood shingles, terra cotta, glass, and paint; and a formal classicism of Palladian windows and Tuscan columns combined with the informal medievalism of a cylindrical tower topped by a helmet-roofed belvedere.

This house and neighborhood were part of Atlanta's rebirth in the years after the Civil War, when the phoenix became the city's symbol, and *Resurgens* its motto, when Atlanta became the future-oriented capital of the New South. Inman Park developer Joel

Hurt and the builder of this house were both entrepreneurs of the sort that came to Atlanta to join the fray and create such successes as the series of cotton expositions held in the 1880s and 1890s.

One hundred years later, this real estate development of that renaissance became the setting of another rebirth, led by a new breed of vital Victorians from our own era. The Beath-Griggs house was their model and their meeting place in saving their garden suburb from four-lane highways, absentee landlords, governmental neglect, and too many years of insensitivity to the charms of the "rich, picturesque, infinitely varied" Queen Anne architecture of the late nineteenth century, when Atlanta began to form its present character and spirit.

Opposite: Library. The original woodwork survived the division of the house into apartments. The mantelpiece with troubadour tiles, demonstrates the romantic historicism of the Aesthetic Movement. Above: The rear porch has been converted into a solarium with a view of the rear garden and pool.

Nicolson-McCord House, Shellmont Lodge
Walter T. Downing, architect, 1892
Piedmont Avenue, Midtown

WHEN THIS HOUSE was designed and built in the last decade of the nineteenth century, the neighborhood around it was beginning to be developed by Edward C. Peters (1852–1937) on land he had inherited from his father, Richard Peters (1810–1889). Edward Peters had formed the Peters Land Company in 1890. His father, a civil engineer from a prominent Philadelphia family, had come to Atlanta when it was called Marthasville. He came because of railroads, helped change the name of the town to Atlanta, and stayed to become one of its richest business and civic leaders and largest landowners.

Before the Civil War, Richard Peters had purchased all of the land lot of 202.5 acres on which this house was built, Land Lot 49, as well as Land Lot 80, where Georgia Tech was founded in 1888. (Richard Peters paid $5.00 an acre for the 405 acres.)

In 1882 Richard Peters began the original movement into this part of the city—which Atlantans started calling Midtown in the early 1970s as it began to be renovated—when he built his palatial Peachtree Street mansion between Fourth and Fifth streets on a 10-acre block. Many of Atlanta's elite followed suit, among them Dr. William Perrin Nicolson, Sr., who built this house as his home in 1892. Nicolson purchased the land from Edward Peters, who had followed his father's lead by building his own Ivy Hall in 1885 at Piedmont Avenue and Ponce de Leon Avenue

(now the Mansion Restaurant). An important part of the development of the area was Peters's Atlanta Street Railroad Company, especially the extension of the Peachtree Street Line in 1891 and then in 1893, two blocks east, the Piedmont Avenue Line.

Dr. Nicolson was one of the first residents attracted to the Peters Land Company development east of Peachtree; he was a professor at the Atlanta College of Physicians and Surgeons, which became in 1915 the medical department of Emory University. Dr. Nicolson's architect was Walter T. Downing (1865–1918), perhaps Atlanta's preeminent residential architect before Neel Reid. Downing had just begun his practice, and this was one of his first house designs. Born

in Boston, but reared in Atlanta, Downing studied architecture under the old apprentice system with the learned L. B. Wheeler (1854–1899), designer of the Kimball House II. Downing was a late-Victorian classicist, vigorously and eclectically experimenting with numerous styles, but especially with Renaissance classicism. The book of house photographs and plans he published in 1897, *Domestic Architecture*, is one of the most interesting records of Atlanta in that era. (A rare book indeed today, it illustrates the W. P. Nicolson house on pages 37, 39, 41, and 138.)

This house is the best preserved of his designs. It has been in the hands of only two families, the Nicolsons and, more recently, the McCords. Since 1892

Opposite: Entrance elevation facing Piedmont Avenue. Above: The living hall and stair well of the Nicolson-McCord house have been meticulously restored and feature original overmantel details, woodwork, and stained glass windows.

several generations of Nicolsons have resided here, making almost no changes in the house or carriage house, even after neighborhood houses were converted to apartments and boardinghouses, and sometimes much less savory places, before the revival of the area had begun. In the July 1973 *Atlanta* magazine Robert Lowery Nicolson explained why his family intended to continue to live in their home place:

"This part of Atlanta was farmland not long ago. I remember hunting in back of the house and I remember them taking up the streetcar tracks. No, there's too many memories here, too much history. A little problem here and there in the neighborhood won't make me leave."

Contractor Edward McCord and his wife Debbie purchased the house from the Nicolson estate in 1982. They have carefully restored it as their home and bed and breakfast lodge. It is a virtual museum of the Victorian era in Atlanta, the period out of which the city has grown and prospered and in which its spirit was formed. The McCords join the Peterses, the Nicolsons, and Walter Downing in furthering the classic Atlanta Spirit.

BLOUNT HOUSE
Architect unknown, 1910;
Restoration architect, Thomas A. Blount, 1987–88;
Myrtle Street, Midtown

THE NAME MIDTOWN began to be used in the early 1970s to refer to a rather sizeable arrowhead-shaped area pointing north toward Buckhead. The area extends along either side of Peachtree Street roughly from North Avenue on the south to Rhodes Hall (1903) on the north (the point of the arrowhead), from Monroe Drive on the east, to I-75/85 on the west. The designation Midtown has come to encompass Colony Square (1969) at Peachtree and Fourteenth streets, Piedmont Park (1904), the Piedmont Driving Club (1887 and 1963), Memorial Arts Center (1968), and theaters, churches, apartment buildings, banks, skyscrapers and other business buildings, restaurants, stores, and shops, and two residential neighborhoods: Ansley Park (1904) and the less-defined district along Piedmont Avenue, Myrtle Street, and Penn Avenue, and the numbered streets from Fourth to Tenth, which the Atlanta Urban Design Commission has demarcated as the Midtown Urban Conservation District (c. 1885–c. 1930s).

This house on Myrtle Street represents the ongoing renovation of Midtown, whose origins are usually traced to the architect Henri Jova's family compound on Mentelle Drive at Seventh Street. Certainly the best-known

Opposite: Entrance elevation facing Myrtle Street.
Above: Kitchen addition and courtyard.

urban pioneer in the area, Mr. Jova recalled for *Atlanta* magazine in 1973, "When I moved to Mentelle Drive in 1958 I had no delusions of saving a neighborhood; all I wanted was the cheapest, rattiest place I could find." The townhouse complex he began creating in 1958 out of an existing duplex set a precedent for possibilities in remodeling and renovation. By the 1970s so much had been achieved that

a Midtown Neighborhood Association was incorporated to provide a forum for leadership and, since there were enough renovations, to sponsor a tour of homes.

In April 1989 Joseph Blount's house was ready for that annual tour. He began his renovation in the late spring of 1987. Edward McCord, in the nearby W. P. Nicolson house, was his engineer-contractor. In 1989, after the

house was ready for the tour, McCord reminisced, "It was deplorable, absolutely the worst house I've ever been in; absolutely uninhabitable." At that time Joe Blount also recalled, "Originally, the house was a two-story, twenty-room building with 4,800 square feet done in plain, Victorian style, not even Queen Anne. It had been a boardinghouse for twenty-five years and was a major sore spot for

Blount House

Above left: Living room-study.
Above: Entrance-stair hall looking
through to dining room.

the neighborhood." Blount already owned a house on Myrtle. He and a group of residents petitioned the city and finally had the place closed down in May 1987. Blount bought it because it would protect his original investment; it was a bargain, and he especially liked the double front porches that wrapped around the corner overlooking Fifth Street.

Repairing the deplorably deteriorated structure began in July 1987 and ended in June 1988 when Blount moved in. His brother, Thomas A. Blount, was his architect. Ed McCord

practically gutted and then rebuilt the interior "works." Amazingly, under thirty years of grime, they found beautifully wrought brass hardware, artglass windows, even chandeliers, still intact. Because Blount and his business partner and housemate Luis A. Garcia enjoy cooking, they wanted the kitchen to be entirely new and spacious and open to the light. Tall windows overlook the back courtyard-garden designed by Atlanta landscape architect Dan Franklin, who also planned the front and side yards for the lowest possible maintenance.

Midtown was once considered suburban, but today it is entirely urban. Joe Blount wanted an in-town, urban house and garden. To help with interior decorating Blount employed a professional decorator, Suzanne B. Allen, but both he and Garcia have definite, informed, and colorful taste that they exercise daily in their furnishings business.

In remaking this former boardinghouse into their home, Garcia, originally of Guatemala, and Blount, originally of Alabama, are new leaders in the revival of Midtown. The Atlanta Spirit of *Resurgens* lives at 781 Myrtle Street.

Blount House

Martin Luther King, Jr., Birth Home
Architect unknown, 1895
501 Auburn Avenue, "Sweet Auburn," East Side

AMERICANS OF AFRICAN DESCENT have made up a large portion of the Atlanta population for many years, and, despite the history of racial segregation, they have long contributed to the creative and dynamic Atlanta Spirit of community building. This Atlanta Spirit may indeed be recognized in the role of black Atlantans as leaders in the national movement for Civil Rights.

Historically, much of black community and business life in Atlanta has centered on two sides of town, known as the East Side and the West Side, roughly flanking the central business district at Five Points. Essentially, the East Side *is* Auburn Avenue, "Sweet Auburn," the site of the birthplace and grave of Martin Luther King, Jr., his church, Ebenezer Baptist, and the district surrounding these historic sites.

The West Side is essentially the Atlanta University Center, also a historic district, made up of five colleges: Spelman, Morehouse, Clark Atlanta University, Morris Brown, and the Interdenominational Theological

Opposite above: The restored entrance elevation facing Auburn Avenue. Above: Parlor. Left: Dining room.

Martin Luther King Birth Home

The upstairs bedroom where Martin Luther King, Jr., was born January 15, 1929.

Center; the Alonzo Herndon Home; and the adjacent community, now including West End, formerly a predominately white neighborhood. Hunter Street is a major thoroughfare through the West Side.

In 1909 the Reverend A. D. Williams, the maternal grandfather of Martin Luther King, Jr., and pastor of nearby Ebenezer Baptist Church, bought this Queen Anne style fourteen-room frame house built in 1895 for a fireman stationed at the neighborhood firehouse. Here, in the second-floor middle bedroom, on January 15, 1929, the first son of the Reverend Williams's daughter, Alberta, and her husband, Martin Luther King, was born and named for his father.

Martin Luther King, Jr., (1929–1968) lived in this house until he was twelve at which time the family moved to a new home on Boulevard Drive. Within this two-block National Historic Site and Preservation District, established in 1980, is the birthplace, grave site, church, the King Center for Social Change, and related structures in the neighborhood where the Nobel Peace Prize Laureate (1964) grew up, and where his grandfather, his father, and he had preached.

Martin Luther King Birth Home

Reynolds Cottage
Architect unknown, 1900–01
Spelman College, West Side

REYNOLDS WAS BUILT as the home for the presidents of Spelman, the oldest college for black women in the nation. John D. Rockefeller, Jr., the primary benefactor of the college, provided for "the creation of a residence for the president," a notation from his own pen. He also provided money to furnish the cottage, which is, in fact, a twenty-two-room, three-story, late-Victorian red brick mansion. Part of the campus quadrangle, it is next to Sisters' Chapel (1928), named for Mrs. John D. (Laura Spelman) Rockefeller and her sister, Miss Lucy Spelman.

The residence was named for Mary C. Reynolds, corresponding secretary of the Women's Baptist Mission Society. It is part of the Atlanta University Center Historic District, entered into the National Register of Historic Places on July 12, 1976.

Currently the dynamic president of Spelman College, Johnnetta B. Cole, lives at Reynolds Cottage. Presiding in the best tradition of the Atlanta Spirit, Dr. Cole is the first woman to serve on the board of directors of Coca-Cola Enterprises.

Above left: Entrance elevation facing the quadrangle. Above: Parlor of Reynolds Cottage, featuring the African and Caribbean collections of Dr. Johnnetta Cole.

President's Home
Architect unknown, 1933
Clark Atlanta University, West Side

THIS GEORGIAN REVIVAL HOUSE was built in 1933 for the presidents of the first black school in the Atlanta University Center—Atlanta University, which was chartered in 1867 and opened in 1869. Called Clark Atlanta University since the 1989 consolidation with Clark College, Atlanta University was built on a portion of seventy acres of land set aside in the West Side area of Atlanta.

HERNDON HOME
Designer, Adrienne McNeil Herndon, 1910
587 University Place, N.W., West Side

MR. AND MRS. ALONZO F. HERNDON bought property from Atlanta University to erect their spacious West Side home, which commands a splendid view of downtown Atlanta from atop a hill adjoining the Atlanta University Center. Mrs. Herndon, Adrienne McNeil, designed the fifteen-room house in the Beaux-Arts neoclassical style to complement the college context. Completed in 1910, it was largely constructed by black craftsmen led by Will Campbell, a black carpenter.

Mrs. Herndon taught drama and elocution at her alma mater, nearby Atlanta University, but she died from Addison's disease the week that her home was completed. Two years later

Opposite top: Entrance elevation.
Opposite bottom: Entrance hall. Above: Stair hall.

Herndon House

Mr. Herndon married Jessie Gillespie of Chicago.

Alonzo Franklin Herndon (1858–1927) was born a slave in Walton County, Georgia, near Social Circle. By the turn of the century he was the wealthiest black man in Atlanta. Herndon spent his youth in the cotton fields, but he later learned to barber and eventually owned and operated three elegant barbershops in Atlanta. He also had extensive real estate holdings, and in 1905 he organized the Atlanta Mutual Insurance Association, later the Atlanta Life Insurance Company, the largest black-owned stockholder insurance company in the United States.

Norris Bumstead Herndon succeeded his father as president of the company in 1927, and under his lead-

ership it prospered greatly. Norris, a bachelor, lived in the grand house on University Place until his death in 1977, longer than any other member of his family, and many of the furnishings and decorations reflect his taste and travels. In 1950 he established a chari-table foundation that operates the house as a memorial to his family. The Herndons, as leaders of the black com-munity, furthered the Atlanta Spirit in worthy new directions, which continue through Atlanta Life and the Herndon Charitable Foundation.

Top: The frieze in the parlor of the Herndon house illustrates three periods in the life of Alonzo Herndon: slavery, hard work, and success. Opposite: Parlor. Above: Dining room.

Herndon House

IN 1892 JOEL HURT, creator of Inman Park, commissioned a plan by Frederick Law Olmsted for Druid Hills, a suburban development to be located on the beautiful rolling land northeast of downtown Atlanta. In 1908 a consortium headed by Asa Griggs Candler (1851–1929), the founding father of the Coca-Cola Company, paid Hurt $500,000 for the unfinished subdivision.

Six years later Asa Candler gave his brother, Bishop Warren A. Candler of the Methodist Episcopal Church South, a check for $1,000,000 and a seventy-five-acre section of Druid Hills to encourage the founding of Emory University. Emory College, the Methodist school at Oxford, Georgia, became the namesake, the undergraduate division, and the parent institution, moving to the campus in Druid Hills in 1919.

In the meantime, Druid Hills had become somewhat of a Candler estate. In 1916 Asa Candler moved from Callan Castle (1902), his home in Inman Park, into a new house on Ponce de Leon Avenue, overlooking the long and winding Olmsted-planned park that dominates the landscape of southern Druid Hills. That same year, Charles Howard Candler became the new president of his father's company and began planning his own country manor not far away on Briarcliff Road.

For their architect, Charles and Flora Glenn Candler chose Henry Hornbostel (1867–1961), who had been associated with the Candler family through the Coca-Cola Company since sometime before 1915, when he produced the master plan for the new Emory University. Hornbostel studied at Columbia University and at the École des Beaux-Arts in Paris, where he was a gifted draftsman known for his per-spective sketches. In 1904 he founded the Department of Architecture at the Carnegie Institute in Pittsburgh after winning the competition for the design of the campus.

That the Candlers (Charles and later his brother Walter Turner Candler at Lullwater, 1925–26) commissioned Tudor Revival country houses is. probably due in part to the sylvan setting of Druid Hills. The English country house, which began its central role in the cultural life of England in the Tudor period, usually represented the life of several generations. As styles changed, the country house evolved, sometimes only a room at a time, reflecting new generations of taste.

Hornbostel's design in 1917 for Callanwolde represents just such an evolution, while faithfully following the precepts of academic eclecticism he had learned at the École. The character of the interior is Tudor with a decidedly Beaux-Arts flavor, especially the staircase, and the dining room appears as if it had been redecorated by an Italian Renaissance ancestor.

Callanwolde was originally the manor house on twenty-seven acres; today there are twelve and it is a DeKalb County fine arts center operated by the Callanwolde Foundation. The name Callanwolde derives from the Candler family's origins in Kilkenny, Ireland, at Callan Castle. *Wold* is from the Old English *weald* or *wold* meaning originally forest, now rolling plain .

Right: Front elevation. Above: Candler coat of arms: Ad Mortem Fidelis *"faithful to the death."*

Above: Dining room. Opposite: Great hall and staircase.

IN 1977 ALISTAIR COOKE, the famous British lecturer and writer, visited Emory University and proclaimed the campus "the most beautiful in America." Cooke was taken with Emory's "plunging hills and gardens and little lakes, all set off with towering trees," and concluded, "visiting Emory was like walking into the Garden of Eden."

Certainly the Druid Hills landscape that captivated the Englishman Cooke had also inspired Walter Turner Candler (1885–1967), the fourth child of Asa Griggs Candler, to charge young architect Lewis Crook with the task of creating a manor house compatible with its parklike surroundings. Crook's response was an academic eclectic interpretation of the domestic architecture of Tudor England (with pre-Tudor and post-Tudor features).

In the Tudor period, defensive features such as castellated towers and fortified gateways were still being erected but for ornament rather than warfare. They had become symbols of the manorial power of the lord or squire. Compton Wynyates (c. 1520), close to perfection as a model of these Tudor Gothic manors, itself an example

LULLWATER HOUSE
Architect, Lewis E. Crook, Jr.,
Ivey & Crook, 1925–26
1483 Clifton Road,
Emory University, Druid Hills

Top: Entrance elevation.
Above: Main entrance.
Opposite: Entrance-stair hall.

of revivalism, was inspirational in the early twentieth-century revival of the style by professional architects. (Some of England's first professional architects appeared during the Tudor period, among them Robert Smythson, one of the creators of the great "prodigy houses.")

Lullwater House, sited on a hill above a twelve-acre lake formed from South Peachtree Creek, features a prominent castellated tower and half-timbered projections relieving an exterior surface of locally quarried fieldstone. On the interior, designer Crook, true to the inspiration of early English country houses, evokes a feeling that the house evolved over several stylistic periods. The English Renaissance style entrance-stair hall appears to date from the late seventeenth century, while the living room is reminiscent of a "long gallery" in a Tudor period house.

With 7,500 square feet of living space, the great house was the focus of a 185-acre estate when Walter Candler made Lullwater Farms his home. Still truly a manorial symbol, Lullwater House has been the home of the presidents of Emory University since 1963.

Lullwater House

GLENN HOUSE, GLENRIDGE HALL
Architects, Cooper & Cooper, 1929
North Fulton County, Sandy Springs

THE COUNTRY HOUSE became a center of English social life and culture in the late Middle Ages. Glenridge Hall partakes of a tradition that began in England 450 years ago, in the fifteenth and sixteenth centuries, when the Tudor kings helped make possible a more peaceful countryside. By the gradual suppression of disorder, the Tudors reduced the need for the massive walls and other trappings of castles, although crenelated battlements and towers and fortified gateways remained in favor as decorative elements. In the days of Henry VIII (1491–1547), bricks and half-timbering became more common than rock masonry, windows were larger and filled with glass, and great sheltering roofs, punctuated with tall ornamented chimneys, covered the rambling, asymmetrical manor houses that Glenridge resembles.

In the same category as ornamental battlements, towers, and gateways were great halls, which had been central architectural elements in England since Roman times. Much of medieval life was lived in common in such halls. As the Tudor period reached its climax in the reign of Henry VIII's daughter, Elizabeth I (1558–1603), great halls had become symbolic of what English-speaking people understood to mean house and home.

By the Tudor period, although the lord of the manor rarely dined in the great hall with his feudal retainers, that soaring manorial space remained as a symbol of the lord's power and place in the countryside; it had evolved into a much-embellished chamber displaying panelled walls, great bay windows, carved fireplaces, and highly ornamented timber roofs. The greater the hall, in theory, the greater the family. This was the tradition in which Glenridge was built.

Clearly the Tudor period reflected a profound veneration for the past, yet a great confidence in the future. The Atlanta Spirit and that of the Tudors

have much in common. T. K. Glenn's position in his community was not unlike that of a great lord. It was only fitting that in 1929 he should have built a Tudor Revival country house with a magnificent great hall for himself and his lady, Elizabeth Ewing Glenn. In 1929 financiers such as Glenn had just completed a booming era of business, and their confidence in the future was soon to be put to its most severe test—the Great Depression was about to begin. Glenridge, in fact, was completed in October during the very month of the crash.

Thomas Kearney Glenn, born in Mississippi and raised in Georgia, came to Atlanta in 1887. Within four years he became an associate of Joel Hurt, one of Atlanta's greatest citizens, in Hurt's Atlanta Consolidated Street Railway

Company, and began a pattern of greatness himself, eventually heading or serving on the boards of several of the city's largest and most successful companies.

Glenn's sister, Flora Glenn Candler (with whom he built Glenn Memorial Church at Emory in 1931), was the wife of Charles Howard Candler, chairman of the board of Coca-Cola. The Candlers, of course, lived in the great Tudor Revival Callanwolde in Druid Hills. Glenn family legend has it that when Glenridge Hall was built it was intended to outshine Callanwolde.

The architect of Glenridge Hall was Samuel Inman Cooper (1894–1974), FAIA, of Cooper & Cooper, formed with his only brother, Joseph Walter Cooper, Jr. (1899–1972), in 1925. Sam Cooper was an Atlanta native, a grand-

son of Samuel M. Inman, and a Princeton graduate. His architecture degree was from the University of Pennsylvania, where he was a student of the great design teacher Paul Cret. Sam Cooper was the firm's designer, his brother the businessman wrote all of the specifications. Sam Cooper once expressed his design credo quite simply: "A building is a merging of art and function; it is more than a visual impression on the beholder. It is primarily for a purpose, often a useful purpose."

Glenridge Hall's original purpose was to serve as a summer country estate for the Glenns; their permanent home was a penthouse in the Biltmore

Opposite: Entrance elevation.
Above: Garden elevation.

Glenridge Hall

Opposite: Great hall. Above: Inglenook in great hall.

Apartments a block off Peachtree Street on Fifth Street. Glenridge became a self-sufficient 400-acre working farm with an estate staff of nearly thirty. At that time—before Georgia 400 and the extension of Abernathy Road—it was reached from Roswell Road via winding Glenridge Road, then by way of a long and picturesque estate road that followed the contours of the heavily forested land until, upon arrival, it was, indeed, as though the twentieth century had been lost and the sixteenth century found.

After T. K. Glenn's death the family eventually sold much of the estate, and the house itself was in peril. But the Hall was saved and restoration work began because of what the *Atlanta Constitution* (May 8, 1983) called "the stubbornness of T. K. Glenn's only granddaughter," Frances Glenn Mayson. Frances and her fiancé, Joseph Mayson, persuaded the family to retain the present acreage and house, and in May 1980, after they were married, the couple moved into the house and began its rehabilitation. She was the first family mem-

ber to live there since 1950. (From 1953 to 1964 the Westminster Schools of Atlanta leased both the Hall and staff house as dormitories for three faculty families and teenaged students.)

In September 1987, the day after the birth of the Maysons' first child, Frances Glenn Mayson died of complications. The new life of the Hall was suddenly both stilled and renewed when Glenridge became the home of daughter Caroline Glenn Mayson.

Joey Mayson is continuing restoration of the house and grounds in memory of his wife, her father, and her grandfather. That the house should prevail is much in the spirit of the Tudor period: respect for the past, with confidence in the future. As the late Frances Glenn Mayson said in 1983, "I told my father if we didn't save the place, that essentially our family would cease to be, and he agreed."

97   *Glenridge Hall*

IN 1904 AMOS GILES RHODES (1850–1928) moved into his grand new home on the Peachtree Street frontage of his 114-acre estate. His property, more than one-half of a land lot, was only slightly smaller than the adjacent garden suburb of Ansley Park being developed by Colonel Edwin P. Ansley. Rhodes Hall and Ansley Park thrive almost a century later, good neighbors in the area called Midtown.

A. G. Rhodes lived here until his death in 1928. By then Peachtree had begun to be a less fashionable residential address, but for at least two generations it had been *the* street in Atlanta on which to build a mansion. Rhodes, a native of Kentucky, arrived in the New South city of Atlanta in 1874 to make his fortune, and he soon became one of the city's richest businessmen; among the enterprises he headed, A. G. Rhodes & Sons was one of the nation's largest furniture store chains. He and his wife, Amanda Dougherty (1847–1927), made many contributions to the community. The Peachtree Christian Church was built on a portion of their land just north on Peachtree Street at Spring Street.

A year after Rhodes's death, his children, Joseph Rhodes and Louana Rhodes Bricker, respecting their father's desire to preserve his home, deeded his residence and the immediate grounds to the state of Georgia, with the restriction that the state always use the property for historical and educational purposes. Officially named Rhodes Memorial Hall in 1930, it served as the principal State Archives building from then until 1965 and has never ceased serving the people of Atlanta and Georgia as the Rhodes family intended.

Today Rhodes Hall sits on less than an acre—much of the original property lies under the concrete and busy traffic of Spring Street and the I-75/85 expressway—and its carriage house, servants quarters, and stables are no longer standing. In 1937 and 1938 the Rhodes heirs developed Rhodes Center on the north, west, and south sides of the house. The Atlanta firm of Ivey & Crook designed the center in a modern classical style, a restrained background for the house; it was the first shopping center in the city and has served Ansley Park well for many years.

Rhodes's architect was Willis F. Denny II (1877–1905). This was one of Denny's last, finest, and most original designs, and it remains the best preserved reminder of the opulent mansions that once lined either side of Peachtree Ridge from downtown to Buckhead. Built of Stone Mountain granite, Rhodes's distinctive Bavarian castle expressed the beginnings of academic eclecticism in the early twentieth century. An exact style designation is difficult, although some see the influence of H. H. Richardson's Romanesque Revival, especially in the Syrian arches of the veranda and *porte cochere* and in the choice of bold granite building blocks.

Nevertheless, inside and out, Rhodes Hall points to the future of domestic architecture in the first half of our century rather than to the Victorian past. Design was changing as it began to become the realm of traditionalists such as Neel Reid, who worked for Denny in 1904 as this house was being completed. The initial impression of the massive, asymmetrical exterior, topped with battlements and punctuated with towers and turrets, is perhaps misleading, because the house is a highly disciplined design reflecting the new interest in a more accurate rendering of traditional details. On the principal

floor, Denny's academic eclecticism mixes eighteenth-century French elements in the parlor, with a grand reception hall based on various Italian Renaissance styles, and a dining room that combines a more late-Victorian palette inspired by the Arts and Crafts movement.

Above: Entrance elevation facing Peachtree Street. Opposite: Porte cochere detail.

The second-floor bedchambers (the third floor has a smoking room and a billiard room) were reached by one of the most intriguing features of the mansion, an intricately hand-carved Honduran mahogany staircase and nine stairwell panels of painted glass representing *The Rise and Fall of the Confed-* *eracy.* This series was executed in 1904 and 1905 to fill the two-story semicylindrical bay off the reception hall. The Von Gerichten Art Glass Company of Columbus, Ohio, a subsidiary of a German firm, created and installed this extraordinary panorama that rivals the Atlanta Cyclorama painting in its depic- tion of Confederate lore and history. Among the Confederate leaders and generals easily recognized as Georgians are Alexander Stephens, Robert Toombs, Howell Cobb, John B. Gordon, and James Longstreet.

Since 1983 Rhodes Hall has been the state headquarters of the Georgia

Trust for Historic Preservation. As the restoration of Rhodes Hall proceeds toward completion in the 1990s, it represents a triumph of the partnership between the State of Georgia and the Georgia Trust—and one of the Trust's finest historic preservation accomplishments practically in the teeth of an omnivorous building boom. Together, the state and the Trust are preserving, restoring, and protecting the architectural integrity of this early twentieth-century landmark on its high-profile, tree-shaded Peachtree Street site at Ansley Park in Midtown.

Above: Reception Hall looking into dining room (left) and parlor. Rhodes Hall had gas and electric lighting, some of it combined in one fixture. On panels in the walls are a series of oil paintings that A. G. Rhodes commissioned by American artist Lorenzo Coppedge. Opposite below: Honduran mahogany staircase with painted glass windows depicting The Rise and Fall of the Confederacy. *Opposite above, from left: The three* Rise and Fall of the Confederacy *panels include the seals of the ten Confederate states, plus those of the border states of Kentucky (Rhodes's home state), Missouri, and Arkansas; portrait medallions of fifteen Confederate heroes; and vignettes of a hopeful soldier off to war in 1861 and his return to ruins in 1865. Sunrise: President Jefferson Davis takes his oath of office. Noon: General Stonewall Jackson at the First Battle of Manassas. Sunset: General Robert E. Lee, astride Traveller, bids farewell to his troops at Appomattox, Virginia, April 9, 1865.*

Rhodes Hall

ON THE WESTERN EDGE of Ansley Park in the 1910s and 1920s, along either side of Peachtree Street from the vicinity of Fourteenth Street north to Peachtree Circle at Rhodes Hall, apartment buildings—interspersed among fashionable residences and churches—became some of Atlanta's most stylish places of residence. On Peachtree at Sixteenth Street stands one of the buildings that has remained among the most desirable of these, the nine-story Georgian Revival Garrison, called the Reid House condominiums since its award-winning renovation in 1974. (Others were The Virginian [1911]; the St. George [1924]; the Peachtree Terrace [1925]; and the Pershing Point [1925]—by 1986 all had been demolished.)

The property on which the Reid House was constructed in 1924 was part of 202.5-acre Land Lot 105, which an original settler of Fulton County, George Washington Collier, acquired in 1847, lived on and farmed until his death in 1903. Collier lived into his ninetieth year in a simple, frame farmhouse, still surviving just northeast of here in what is now Sherwood Forest, a 1950s subdivision.

In 1904 the city council added Land Lot 105 to the city as the Eighth Ward, containing Piedmont Park on the Piedmont Avenue eastern edge of the lot. At that time the Collier Property began to be sold and subdivided. One of the original purchasers of much of the acreage was E. P. Ansley. He planned, developed, and named Ansley Park,

first calling it Peachtree Garden, to indicate, as he wrote in a prospectus of 1915, the "residential paradise" he and his landscape engineers were creating: "Magnificent roadways wind in and out among groves, parks, and lawns. Mansions surmount the hilltops, bungalows dot the vales. We have preserved the sylvan beauty of the woodland tract, and as a crowning touch have added golf links, playgrounds for children, and a golf club house." In *Atlanta and Environs* (1954) the city's exceptional historian-chronicler, Franklin M. Garrett, wrote: "By 1920 Ansley Park was in full flower as a sought-after residential area. Peachtree Circle, LaFayette Drive, Westminster Drive, Inman Circle, Seventeenth Street, The Prado, were all distinguished by the homes of Atlanta's

solid business and professional men." Franklin Garrett might have included Peachtree Street in his list of some of the most desirable addresses, since, on its western boundary, Ansley Park extended up to and across Peachtree Street to West Peachtree.

Many of the neighborhood's special characteristics survived into the 1970s, the integrity of its architecture and landscape plan as well as the public-spirited character of its residents. The Ansley Park Civic Association, dating back to a few years after 1904, was able to have the area listed in the National Register of Historic Places in 1979 as a historic district. (Unfortunately the Peachtree Street stretch, where this apartment condominium stands, had to be excluded because of intrusions, but subsequently the Reid House was listed in the register in its own right and given local landmark status.)

Top: Entrance façade on Peachtree Street. Opposite: Parlor. Above: Entrance hall looking into parlor.

In June 1926 the Ansley Park neighborhood took on some of the distinctive traits it has retained over the years, even after much building and demolition during the 1960s, 1970s, and 1980s—including construction of a MARTA Station on West Peachtree. At that time Mrs. Joseph M. High gave her Tudor Revival home on a hill on the west side of Peachtree, just north of Fifteenth Street, to the Atlanta Art Association to house the High Museum of Art. Her house was long ago replaced by the Arts Center and the new High Museum, but Mrs. High's bequest insured that this close-in suburban neighborhood would become the focus of many of the city's artistic and cultural activities and continue to make it much sought-after.

All through the changes in this area, which was called Uptown for a brief time and finally Midtown in the early 1970s, Ansley Park remained the picturesque garden suburb it was planned to be—with only a sprinkling of genteel boarding houses suggesting the northward movement of Atlantans to newer suburbs.

Along that sophisticated stretch of Ansley Park-Peachtree: from Colony Square (1968), past the petite Pershing Point Memorial Park (1920), and extending to Rhodes Hall (1904), stands the Reid House, a true bastion of classic Atlanta.

Overlooking Peachtree, the two-level apartment of George Lanier, Esq., designed by Eugene Surber and decorated by David Byers, reflects the Georgian Revival style of the Reid House set by Hentz, Reid & Adler's Neel Reid and Philip Shutze over sixty-five years ago. It carries forward a stylish old tradition of Peachtree Street-Ansley Park apartment living, but with the contemporary twist that Mr. Lanier's apartment is truly his home, because it is a condominium. The main floor of the apartment contains the entrance hall, living room, library-dining room, solarium, and kitchen. The bedroom suite, a wine cellar, and service area on the lower level are reached by a staircase decorated by the work of Georgia ironmaster Ivan Bailey.

Among the many stylistic elements that Messrs. Lanier, Surber, and Byers used to create a unique living environment is a Pompeian mural that decorates the solarium. Painted by Susan Roberts, an Athens artist on the University of Georgia faculty, the room reflects Lanier's love of classical taste and traditions and exotic locales.

Solarium and library-dining room. The Pompeian mural is by Susan Roberts.

Reid House

GRANT-JONES HOUSE
Architect, Lewis E. Crook, Jr., Ivey & Crook, 1948
Peachtree Circle, Ansley Park

WHEN THIS HOUSE WAS BUILT in the late 1940s, one block off Peachtree Street and around the corner from the Reid House, few architects still designed in the classical tradition, and few dwellings of any kind and style were being built in this historic old neighborhood. Developed beginning in 1904 as a garden suburb—once called an "automobile suburb" because it was Atlanta's first after motor cars began to be generally available—Ansley Park was considered by 1950 to be hopelessly old-fashioned; few building sites remained, and the present Midtown concept of in-town living had not yet evolved. But there were exceptions and this Peachtree Circle home is one of the most appealing residences built at any time in the long history of the venerable neighborhood.

Designed by Lewis Edmund Crook, Jr., of the Atlanta architectural firm of Ivey & Crook, this red-brick classical house was built as the home of Lawrence E. Grant, a real estate investor whose ancestor, the civil engineer Lemuel P. Grant (1817–1893), gave the land for Atlanta's Grant Park. Buck Crook (1898–1967) was one of

Atlanta's best classicists; he and his partner, Ernest Ivey, were among the last Atlanta architects to continue a traditional practice when large offices and modernism had become the fashion. They had met as employees at Hentz, Reid & Adler, forming their partnership in 1923 in the mold of that exceptional firm. Up until both partners died in the mid-1960s, they designed (Crook) and supervised the construction of (Ivey) some of the South's finest structures in the traditional styles: houses, churches, business and college buildings—some forty for Emory University. Their buildings are still highly prized as well-planned works of architecture with timeless qualities of proportion, scale, craftsmanship, taste in ornamentation, interior space distribution, and siting.

There is no better example of their work than this perfect gem of classicism in its leafy Ansley Park setting overlooking Winn Park. (To the south is the Henry de Give house, c. 1911, one of the city's few examples of the sweepingly horizontal Prairie School of early modernism.) The Roman Ionic porch and fanlighted doorway, approached through a green lawn by way

of a straight walkway from the sidewalk, are Jeffersonian: crisp white classical trim contrasting with warm red bricks and cool black-green shutters. Formal in plan, a wide central hallway is flanked by a living room and dining room freshly decorated by Mel Hammock for Dr. George Winford Jones, Jr., the owner since 1986. The living room is especially handsome, with a fine Adam mantelpiece and panelled bookshelves and an entrance to a side garden on the south side of the house.

Crook's one-story classical revival evocation for Lawrence Grant architecturally symbolizes Ansley Park's timeless desirability as an old planned suburb near downtown. An exception when it was built just after World War II, this house is another one of the factors that allowed Ansley Park to be listed as a district—a high accolade for the old neighborhood—on the National Register of Historic Places in 1979 only seventy-five years after its founding.

Above: Front elevation. Opposite: Living room and library-sitting room. Opposite top: Central entrance hall looking into living room.

Grant-Jones House

ON A PORTION OF LAND LOT 110 in the Andrew Jackson Collier estate, Ben Franklin Burdett and Arthur C. Burdett began their development of Brookwood Hills in the early 1920s; the civil engineer O. F. Kaufman laid out the wooded neighborhood, some sixty-five rolling acres, with houses restricted to at least $10,000 in cost. (These same houses today change hands for fifty times that.)

Even today, thanks largely to an old and ever-active neighborhood civic association, there are no through streets and few intrusions, even on the Peachtree Street boundary of this handsome cul-de-sac of family homes. (Peachtree Street becomes Peachtree Road at Palisades, one of the main streets of the neighborhood.) At the heart of the area are a community clubhouse and swimming pool, Burdett Park, named for the family that so thoughtfully developed the subdivision—even planting the oak trees that still line the roadways and shade the wide sidewalks.

In 1928 the William A. Parkers built this Georgian Revival house on a Brighton Road elevation that today is the home of Anne and Bradley Hale. The Hales purchased the place from Mr. and Mrs. William A. Parker, Jr., in the fall of 1964, because, as Anne Sheffield Hale said, "The house looked like Thanksgiving and Christmas." They did very little to the house, adding only air conditioning, repairing plaster, strip-

Above:: Detail of doorway looking into entrance-stair hall. Opposite top: Entrance elevation facing Brighton Road. Opposite: Living room.

ping the woodwork of many coats of paint before repainting, and adding a side door to the garden.

The original plans of the house are in the Ivey & Crook Collection of the Atlanta Historical Society. Several years after the house was completed Buck Crook designed for the Parkers a library-den. Otherwise the house is es-

sentially as shown in the original working drawings. The Hales had the front landscape and rear garden recast by landscape architect Edward L. Daugherty, FASLA, in the 1960s.

Buck Crook's timeless Georgian Revival design for the Parkers, now lovingly appreciated and tended by the Hales, was based on an eighteenth-century house on Richmond Hill in the picturesque London borough of Richmond upon Thames, the Wick, still standing as built for Lady St. Aubyn in 1775. Crook owned two books that illustrated the Wick: *Small Houses of the Late Georgian Period* (1923) and *The Smaller English House of the Later Renaissance* (1925). The Parker-Hale house is, of course, not an exact copy of The Wick, either inside or out, but a well-studied improvisation on the theme of a house from the late Georgian period. Many houses in Brookwood Hills were designed by architects. Most of them would have agreed with the authors of *The Smaller English House*, who wrote in 1925: "We are concerned today with the building of moderate sized houses; and it is from the wealth of tradition, both British and American, that *motifs* of plan and composition can be studied."

Atlantans admire neighborhoods composed of such traditionalist or period houses. Brookwood Hills is one of the most classic of such neighborhoods, and this is among the most classical of the houses of Brookwood Hills.

Parker-Hale House

TOMPKINS HOUSE
Architects, Hentz, Reid & Adler, 1922
West Wesley Road, Peachtree Heights Park

"THIS IS ONE of the most complete remaining examples of a Reid villa. It has been lived in by the original owners for fifty years with all intentions of Reid's designs understood." So wrote Professor James Grady in his *Architecture of Neel Reid in Georgia*, published in 1973. In 1991 this tradition still prevails; the widow of Reid's client still resides here, obviously understanding and preserving the "intentions of Reid's designs."

The Tompkins house, with its complementary grounds and gardens, reveals to us the vision Neel Reid of Hentz, Reid & Adler had in housing the Atlanta Spirit more than a half century ago. If today's Atlanta aspires to be "international," it is not because the city has suddenly thought in such terms. This small, yet dignified and sophisticated—even monumental—Anglo-Palladian manor tells us about the city's earlier aspirations to belong to a greater world, to identify with a larger, older, less provincial culture than one might have expected to find in Fulton County, Georgia.

This is classic Buckhead, sited on a

Top: Entrance elevation facing West Wesley Road. Above: Entrance detail. Opposite: Entrance rotunda.

hill, a pedimented pavilion with a formal, large-scale entrance doorway, baroque in character, and a formal rear garden on axis with the library, and, above the garden, a classical white frame service building, quite in the spirit of Palladio, containing a garage, servants' rooms, and laundry—now a guest house.

This villa in Peachtree Heights Park proves, if any proof is needed, that Hentz, Reid & Adler's chief designer, Neel Reid, knew how to orchestrate the design of a complete suburban villa, with all its exterior proportional parts in place and with dramatic interior spatial and decorative effects serving delightful architectural as well as humane ends. Atlanta's long reputation as a city of gracious living may be understood; this is convincing and beautiful evidence.

Neel Reid's first interest was the site and setting. Starting with the grounds, the formality he usually wanted was expressed and carried throughout. He was a master of scale; each element in the design, from the grandly scaled entrance doorway to

the rear garden and temple above, expresses the essence of his style. The small, gracefully sculpted entrance rotunda offers a charming welcome to the intimate scale and beautiful details of the interior.

The house, inside and out, remains essentially as the architect and client conceived it. The owners have preserved it "with all intentions of Reid's designs understood."

But in 1922 Reid had only a few more years to work his magic; in February 1926 at age forty he died of a brain tumor. His reputation among his

Opposite top: Living room. Opposite bottom: Living room chimney breast. Above: Dining room.

contemporaries was aptly expressed in an obituary by Ernest D. Ivey in the *Journal of The American Institute of Architects.* ("Ed" Ivey of Ivey & Crook had worked with Hentz, Reid & Adler for many years before establishing with Lewis Edmund "Buck" Crook, another Reid associate, their mightily successful firm.) Ivey wrote: "In all his work he did not consider his jobs complete until the last shrub was planted in proper relation and the last bit of interior decoration was handled in his own happy style." In those few words, Ernest Ivey summed up Reid's reputation as a complete designer. And Ivey added: "He had an unusual faculty of inspiring all workers connected with any project, from draftsmen to the last workman upon the building, with an unusual *esprit de corps*, and conse-

quent pride in the final result as an artistic achievement."

Writing about Neel Reid in 1926, Ivey speaks to us today: "In his passing he leaves works which may be considered not only monuments to his taste and genius of expression, but which will endure as inspiration for generations to come."

Rightly so, the Tompkins house is a monument to Neel Reid; it is certainly an enduring inspiration to those in present and future generations who would aspire to make Atlanta a great world-class city. Reid and his client Henry Tompkins laid down the gauntlet in 1922; will their work in the classical tradition inspire us to equal or greater heights of creativity? Will our international city be graced by works of architecture as beautiful and sophisticated?

Tompkins House

Above: Solarium. Below: Library looking into garden.

Above: Garden with service pavilion. Below: Garden elevation.

CALHOUN-THORNWELL HOUSE
Architects, Hentz, Reid & Adler, 1922-23
Pinestream Road, Buckhead

IN HER POPULAR NOVEL *Peachtree Road* (1988), Anne Rivers Siddons described Neel Reid as "a classical architect in whom Atlanta has always set great store, whose years abroad studded Northwest Atlanta's wooded hills and ridges with Renaissance, American Georgian, Federal, Greek Revival, Baroque, and Italianate estates of uncommon style and substance." Continuing, she wrote: "At the time most were built, in the late teens and twenties and on into the thirties, entertaining and gardening were two of Old Atlanta's overwhelming passions, and formal receptions and dining rooms and extensive formally landscaped grounds were *de rigueur.*"

Further on in her story Siddons describes a "long, curving . . . ribbon of asphalt that was the driveway to the Pink Castle." That was a nickname Atlantans long ago gave the Calhoun-Thornwell house, but more often calling it a palace instead of a castle. "The Pink Castle," she wrote, "was a great pile . . . of pink stucco and red pantile that lay far out West Paces Ferry Road . . . and had been built vaguely in sixteenth-century Italian style in 1923."

In such a highly romantic myth-and-magnolia account, an Atlanta estate in the mid-1920s had to be single-handedly—down to every garden parterre and interior decorating de-

---

Above: Garden elevation. Aspects of the baroque style were based on the Villa Gori, near Siena, Italy. Opposite: Rear elevation and motor court.

tail—by Neel Reid, who entered the realms of romance himself by dying in 1926 at age forty in the youthful prime of his artistic career.

In fact, however, the firm of Hentz, Reid & Adler was an Atlanta atelier, where many men apprenticed; it was a collaboration of artistic talents and temperaments of varying degrees of experience and training; some men were more aesthetically gifted than others; some more apt to design than engineer, some more prone to sketch, draw, and draft than oversee construction; some more adept at doing business and getting clients than any of the above.

Only in the very earliest days, after Reid and Hal Hentz began the firm together in 1909, was Reid alone the principal designer. By the early 1920s,

his associates and assistants included Philip "Phil" Shutze, Lewis "Buck" Crook, Ernest "Ed" Ivey, and James "Jimmy" Means, all of whom participated in the creation of this estate for Andrew and Mary Trigg Calhoun. In debates about who the principal designer of the Calhoun project may have been, we must not overlook the fact that in the spring of 1922, Neel Reid, already beginning to suffer ill health, and Buck Crook, then only twenty-four and only three years out of Georgia Tech's Department of Architecture, took a four-month trip to England and the continent, including a tour to Italy—following Phil Shutze's Rome Prize path—to see villas used for inspiration in the final design of this and other houses and to buy antiques and other *objets d'art* for the Calhouns and other clients of the firm. (In May 1923 Lewis Crook and Ernest Ivey formed their own firm, Ivey & Crook; one of their initial commissions was to oversee the construction of this estate, listed in their log book, "Supervision for Hentz, Reid & Adler, Andrew Calhoun house.")

At the time the house was built the Calhouns owned the surrounding one hundred acres, developing some eighteen of them formally. Later some of the undeveloped land was used to build Highway 41 to Marietta. Andrew Calhoun (1893–1935) was in real estate, a gentleman farmer, and part of the prominent Atlanta and Georgia branch of the South Carolina Calhouns. His father was Dr. Abner W. Calhoun, the great eye-specialist, and his brother, who continued their father's practice, was Dr. F. Phinizy Calhoun. Here Mrs. Calhoun, Mary Guy Trigg of Chattanooga, Tennessee, founded the Peachtree Garden Club, Atlanta's first, in 1923. The estate, which she named Tryggvesson, included an orchard, a garden, a lake, tennis courts and formal gardens. It was entered through baroque piers on West Paces Ferry, modeled on some that Reid and Crook, and Shutze on an earlier visit, had seen in Verona, Italy, at the Villa Cuzzano. Although these fanciful piers still exist, they have been moved apart to form an entrance to Pinestream Road, built in the valley between West Paces Ferry and the house about 1960, when the terraced gardens and the surrounding acreage were subdivided and developed.

Calhoun-Thornwell House

The Calhouns had five children. A daughter, Louise Calhoun, married Roby Robinson, Jr., and moved to this house some years after her mother was widowed. The Robinsons lived here until about a year before they and over one hundred other Atlantans perished in a tragic air crash at Orly Field in Paris in 1962. In January 1961 Mr. and Mrs. Allison Thornwell, Jr., decided against building a new house and purchased this property—investing in a true Atlanta landmark.

Even now their home has the power to evoke a more romantic era in the city's history when, during the 1920s, the Metropolitan Opera Company came to Atlanta for a season in the spring. Beginning in 1910 and

Above: Drawing room. Two Allyn Cox murals were part of the original decorations of this room, which is now used for dances and formal receptions. Opposite: Stair hall, from the drawing room to the dining room. This hall connects the three principal rooms.

continuing off and on until the early 1980s, Atlantans hosted world-famous musical celebrities such as the Italian-born soprano Galli-Curci and the conductor Arturo Toscanini, who must have felt right at home at post-performance parties in this baroque stucco villa in Buckhead. Sir Rudolf Bing, the late general manager of the Met, reminisced in his *5000 Nights At the Opera*

(1972): "I must admit I enjoyed the visits to Atlanta. Never have I known a place to become so excited about opera: work stopped, sleep stopped all over town while the Metropolitan was there. They sold out the theater months in advance; people lined up for miles and fought to get in."

That was the spirit that built this baroque Pink Palace and this city. Even without its estate intact, this house retains an aura of the spirit that propelled the city toward cosmopolitan and historic achievements. This spirit continues to link Peachtree Street and Road with the rest of the world—the welcome mat is out even though our doorsteps may have become more prosaic, less grandly operatic than this.

119   *Calhoun-Thornwell House*

Opposite: Entrance stair hall. Between the living room and dining room, an original Allyn Cox mural survives. Above: Dining room. Atlanta interior decorator T. Gordon Little redecorated this room around the original moldings, chandelier, fireplace, and the roundel of Michelangelo. Right: Library. Now the main sitting room, the library was redecorated in the 1970s.

Calhoun-Thornwell House

NIXON-WATSON HOUSE
Architect, Neel Reid; Hentz, Reid & Adler, 1926
Andrews Drive, Peachtree Heights Park

ANDREWS DRIVE, named for a founder of Peachtree Heights, follows a winding course northwest to West Paces Ferry Road from Peachtree near West Wesley. The wooded land, sloping east from Andrews toward Peachtree Ridge at Buckhead, provided some of the handsomest building sites in Atlanta. Many of the houses gracing these leafy knolls were designed and supervised by the architectural firm started in 1909 by Hal Hentz and Neel Reid.

This firm, and architects who sprang from it, gave the classic Atlanta Spirit its three-dimensional form. A house by Neel Reid still has a certain aura: "It's a Neel Reid . . . . He made Atlanta beautiful." This house, which can be said to be his last, partakes of that aura, adding to it in a special way.

In the middle of the affluent 1920s, during the prime of Reid's artistic contributions to the classical tradition, and only months after his fortieth birthday, the youthful and popular architect died of a brain tumor just as the Nixon house was completed. Vaughn Nixon

owned the Atlanta Woolen Mill and his wife, Emmy Johnson, was a daughter of one of the founders of the old Chamberlan, Johnson, and DuBose department store in downtown Atlanta. Reid died at his home, antebellum Mimosa Hall in Roswell, only weeks after he had inspected the Nixon's house from a wheelchair, making his final suggestions.

His firm had a great deal of work on the drawing boards, and, because this house was one of the last that Reid himself had seen from conception to

Above: Entrance elevation, atop a knoll facing Andrews Drive.
Opposite: Entrance detail. Below: Garden elevation.

Nixon-Watson House

Above: Entrance-stair hall. Opposite: Library.

completion it has a special place in the Reid legend. In a period of less than twenty years, Reid had helped create a golden age of domestic architecture, a renaissance in the garden suburbs of this Deep South city. Atlanta had been born too late to share in the eighteenth century, yet had made every effort to rectify this in the years just before and just after the First World War.

A coincidence connected with the design of the Nixon-Watson entrance

façade adds new luster to the old lore. Reid's classical precedent for the front of the house, the beautiful Hammond-Harwood house (1773–74) at Annapolis, Maryland, is one of the primary residential landmarks of American Georgian architecture. Its fanlighted, pedimented, and carved doorway is one of the most admired of that classic period, and Reid's version beautifully replicates the original. But the coincidence that adds another facet to the

Reid legend is that Hammond-Harwood was built according to the designs of another gifted architect, William Buckland (1734–1774), who also died at the top of his career in his fortieth year as he, too, completed his last house, the masterpiece Reid found worthy of emulating in Peachtree Heights.

Reid's Vaughn Nixon house, of course, is not a copy of Buckland's elegant precedent; the garden elevation,

Nixon-Watson House

Above: Dining room. Opposite top: Living room.
Opposite bottom: Solarium

for example, is unlike the Annapolis original, and Reid used white stucco where Buckland used red brick. Captured, however, is the spirit of Hammond-Harwood's symmetry, scale, proportions, and details, making the Vaughn Nixon house one of the Reid firm's finest contributions to the continuation of the classical tradition.

The same sentiment that architectural scholar William Pierson expressed about William Buckland of Annapolis could apply to Neel Reid of Atlanta: "One cannot help but wonder what American architecture would have been like if a more kindly fate had permitted this gifted man to live beyond his fortieth year."

This Buckhead estate presently belongs to the Wayne Watsons, who purchased the property, including original furnishings and fixtures selected by Neel Reid, from Mrs. Nixon's heirs in 1964. W. E. Browne Decorat-

ing Company, which the Watsons call on to help maintain the particular character of the house, years ago placed the pair of large oil paintings, bought in Europe by Neel Reid for a house in Macon, in the entrance hall. The Watsons recognize the worth of their "Neel Reid" down to the most minute details. They preserve their landmark in the spirit of its original creators, the Vaughn Nixons and their architect, Neel Reid.

Nixon-Watson House

EDWARD H. INMAN HOUSE, SWAN HOUSE
Architect, Philip Trammell Shutze, 1926–28
3099 Andrews Drive, Buckhead
Atlanta History Center

THE BEGINNINGS of the fashionable Buckhead residential area where Swan House is located date back to the rural simplicities of the 1830s when Hardy Pace established a ferry on the Chattahoochee River and Henry Irby set up a tavern-grocery called Buckhead at the intersection of Peachtree and Roswell roads. Paces Ferry Road (the prefix *West* came later) grew up as a wagon trail from the ferry to the Peachtree village crossroads where Irby had his business and which soon became the center of an election district.

However uncertain we may be of Buckhead's exact boundaries today as its popularity continues, there is no uncertainty about what the name represents in the city's social history, especially since the first decades of this century when the old-fashioned, "countrified" name for the junction of (West) Paces Ferry, Peachtree, and Roswell roads began to designate one of suburban Atlanta's most desirable residential areas.

One hundred years after Pace and Irby's day, Buckhead consisted of a small shopping area around the historic crossroads that served a collection of well-planned residential neighborhoods on either side of Peachtree Ridge. These Buckhead neighborhoods extend from approximately where Peachtree Creek passes under Peachtree Road at E. Rivers Grammar School to the crossing of Lenox Road on the north, and includes areas on either side of West

---

Opposite: Entrance facade with Doric-columned Palladian portico. Above left: Italianate cascade on garden side facing Andrews Drive. Above right: Garden elevation from Andrews Drive.

Paces Ferry Road from the center of Buckhead to the Chattahoochee River, although some would say this might be stretching the designation a bit. The design work of the great landscape architect Frederick Law Olmsted (1822–1903) in Atlanta and elsewhere, especially Atlanta's own Druid Hills, inspired the layout of these neighborhoods, which followed the wooded contours of the Piedmont terrain. Traditionally included in Buckhead were Peachtree Heights Park and Haynes Manor, the Andrews Drive district, and Tuxedo Park, to name only four of the best known.

On Andrews Drive just south of West Paces Ferry Road, only blocks from where it intersects with Peachtree Road, one of the finest Buckhead estates ever developed is preserved as part of the Atlanta Historical Society's thirty-two-acre History Center. Swan House,

Swan House

the crown jewel of the estate, is a masterpiece of early twentieth-century classicism in the style of the early Georgian period (1710–1760).

The Swan House estate was completed for Mr. and Mrs. Edward Hamilton Inman in 1928. Mrs. Inman, Emily Caroline MacDougald, was an admirer of the work of William Kent (1685–1748), his patron Lord Burlington, and their colleagues in the early eighteenth-century English Palladian

school of architecture and taste. She played a major role in planning, furnishing, and developing the estate. It was she who engaged the eminent Atlanta classicist Philip Trammell Shutze (1890–1982) of the firm of Hentz, Adler & Shutze. In the eighteenth-century virtuoso tradition, Shutze designed the entire scheme, laying out the grounds and gardens and detailing important aspects of furnishings.

When the work commenced, the

Inmans were in their mid-forties. Philip Shutze was thirty-six and just becoming a partner in his firm after the death of Neel Reid, the chief designer and Shutze's mentor. The completed Swan House was a masterpiece, a culmination of the domestic architecture of Georgia and a

Opposite: Circular entrance hall, looking from entrance portico into stair hall. Above: Stair hall.

Swan House

Library. This English Renaissance-style room (the Christopher Wren period) was designed by Shutze to compliment the style and color of the carved wood swag above the mantel. This ornate antique carving of fruit and flowers, done in the early eighteenth century in the manner of Grinling Gibbons, was from the Inmans' Ansley Park house. The Shutze designs, which decorate the rest of the library and adorn the other rooms of the house, were executed by the master carver, H. J. Millard.

quintessential example of Georgians' love of beautiful houses and gardens in the classical revival tradition.

The beauty of Shutze's design consists not as much in the details, though they are perfect, but rather in the fine

Above: Sitting room. Called her "Morning Room" by Emily Inman, this formal, yet comfortable room was decorated by Mrs. Inman, Philip Shutze, and Ruby Ross Goodnow Wood, one of the first professional decorators in America and a native of Monticello, Georgia. (Note the carved swans on the Corinthian capitals.) Right: Detail of stair hall looking into sitting room.

adaptation of the various parts to the whole, creating a unity of effect, a sense of proportion and scale, and a complete assimilation of the structure with the physical site out of which it seems to emerge, as though it were an expression of the hillside. Of the exterior, Philip Shutze said: "It is supposed to be an English Kent house, but the cascade in front is pure Italian. I sketched this in an Italian garden about the time of World War I."

The distant view of the house from Andrews Drive, the winding approach through the grounds, and the Palladian portico that shelters the entrance all set the tone of the composition and prepare the visitor for the delightful interi-

ors. The circular entrance hall and the sumptuously detailed stair hall are separated by a screen of Ionic columns. The two areas combine to create a space that during the day is so filled with light it is like a courtyard into which all of the principal first-floor rooms flow. The freestanding spiral staircase is an elegant *tour de force.*

Throughout the house the beautifully detailed architectural elements are of Shutze's design but were brought to reality by the exquisite carving of H. J. Millard, originally of Bath, England, later of Atlanta.

Only three years after the Inmans occupied the house, Edward Inman died of a heart attack. Mrs. Inman con-

Above: Dining room. This room, as are all those on the first floor, is a masterpiece of design and decoration. The Millard-carved mantel, cornice, and overdoor details; the exotic wallpaper and decorative accoutrements; and the pair of swan consoles create an atmosphere that makes this room, perhaps more than any other in the city, a monument to the success of early twentieth-century Atlanta. Left: Dining room detail. The pair of swan consoles, purchased by Mrs. Inman in Bath, England, in 1924 are attributed to Thomas Johnson (1714–1755), a noted London designer and carver of the Chippendale period.

Swan House

tinued to live at Swan House, the name she gave her home, lavishing attention on its fundamental beauty with an English country-house kind of interior decoration, most of which survives, and formal gardening, which also may still be seen much as it was during her lifetime.

In 1966, the year after Mrs. Inman's death, her hope that the estate, with the house, grounds, and furnishings, would become the property of the Atlanta Historical Society, was realized, and, in the spring of 1967, the historical society opened the principal rooms, gardens, and grounds for tours, using bedrooms and service areas as offices.

After a few years the historical society built a functional headquarters as part of its History Center so that the entire house could be shown as though Mrs. Inman were still at home. (She had said three of her legacies were spent making the place as she wanted it.) One by one, previously closed rooms, including Mrs. Inman's bedroom suite, have been put back as they had been originally.

The Atlanta Spirit, an amalgam of the Old South and the New, was created by families such as the Inmans, who came to Atlanta before and after the Civil War and established fortunes. The Inmans were Southern capitalists—city builders, cotton brokers, and propri-

etors of one of the largest and most widely respected businesses of its kind in the world. Edward Inman's uncle Samuel was called "the first citizen of Atlanta." Another uncle, John H. Inman, suggested that Henry Grady speak to the New England Society in New York City in 1886, and the resulting speech, "The New South," became world-famous.

In 1889, when Henry Grady wrote in the *New York Ledger*: "The new South is simply the old South under new conditions," he might have been describing the Inman's Anglo-Palladian estate in Buckhead created a generation later. As Grady wrote in that same article: "Dear to the new South . . . is

the memory of the old regime, its traditions and its history." That is the Atlanta Spirit, "the old South under new conditions," that one finds at Swan House, well-integrated into the overall classicism of Philip Shutze's design, only blocks away from the Buckhead crossing where just one hundred years earlier Henry Irby had his frontier tavern-grocery.

Opposite above: Mrs. Inman's bedroom. Opposite below: Master bath. Above: Formal garden on southern side of the house. The pool and fountain are similar to one at the Villa Cicogna in Lombardy. Left: Porch overlooking formal garden.

Swan House

Goodrum-Abreu-Rushton House
Southern Center for International Studies
Architect, Philip Trammell Shutze, 1931
320 West Paces Ferry Road, Buckhead

WEST PACES FERRY ROAD has been Atlanta's suburban Fifth Avenue since the time of the First World War. From the center of Buckhead west to the Chattahoochee River, it is the "finger-bowl address" from Atlanta's classic period of residential architecture: a twenty-five-year renaissance, from around 1915 to 1940. One of the finest landmarks of that era is this English

Regency style mansion designed in 1929 and completed in the early 1930s for Mrs. James Jefferson Goodrum, the widow May Patterson Goodrum, who married the architect Francis Abreu in 1939. Sometimes called Peacock House, in 1960 it became the home of Mrs. W. W. Rushton and in 1984 the headquarters of the Southern Center for International Studies.

In the four-volume MacMillan *Encyclopedia of Architects* (1982), the architect of this house, Philip Shutze, is only one of two Atlanta architects included; the other is the architect-developer and confirmed modernist John Portman. This house was one of Shutze's favorites, sometimes said to be his most favorite of those in Atlanta. In 1932, soon after it was completed,

Shutze received an honorable mention for its design from the Architectural League of New York, and in July of that year it was featured in *Architecture*, a professional architectural journal published on Fifth Avenue by Charles Scribner's Sons—high recognition for an Atlantan in the days when becoming an international city was farfetched even for those most caught up in the Atlanta Spirit.

On June 17, 1982, only months before his death at age ninety-two, Philip Shutze received another New York accolade, the highest award of the Classical America Society, for a "lifetime devoted to upholding the classical in its finest tradition." Also acknowledged at that time was his life-long colleague and friend, Allyn Cox of New York, the painter of the beautiful chinoiserie murals in the dining room of this house. Shutze and Cox, both Rome Prize winners, had met just before World War I at the American Academy in Rome. This 1930 Atlanta collaboration was one of the landmarks

cited in the Classical America award.

Local statistics connected with this house also aptly demonstrate the esteem in which Atlantans have held it. The Goodrum-Abreu-Rushton house was included in the prestigious, but now discontinued, Henrietta Egleston annual spring tour of homes eight times, more than any other estate. In 1933, the first year of the tour, when the house was hardly more than a few months old, Mrs. Goodrum graciously shared the classic Regency beauty she and Philip Shutze had created. The house was also featured from 1935–1939 and in 1960 and 1968. (A small-scaled, sparely elegant, somewhat exotic version of late-Georgian taste, Regency was one of Shutze's favorite styles.)

When the house was open in 1960 and 1968 on the Egleston Tour, the owner of the property was Mrs. W. W. Rushton, who turned it over to posterity with its architectural integrity intact. The famous Allyn Cox dining room murals are still as fresh, bright, and captivating as they must have been

when he painted them, as are Athos Menaboni's fanciful designs for the octagonal breakfast room. The carved wood details for the living room and entry are by Herbert J. Millard (1884–1978), also a Shutze associate and one of Atlanta's most artistic craftsmen. They too are crisp and clear.

A landmark of Atlanta's early twentieth-century golden age of residential architecture, this estate is preeminent testimony to the beauty of the classical tradition as practiced in Atlanta. The works of such fine firms as Hentz, Reid & Adler, later Hentz, Adler & Shutze, are perhaps the finest artistic legacy of the wealth that Atlanta produced in the first half of the century. While New York's Fifth Avenue has lost most of its residential luster, Atlanta's West Paces Ferry Road has grown in distinction as the heart of the city's most elegant neighborhood.

Opposite: Entrance elevation facing West Paces Ferry Road. Above: Garden elevation.

Above: Dining room with murals by Allyn Cox. Left: Mural detail with entrance hall and living room beyond. Opposite: Breakfast room with painted decoration by Athos Menaboni.

Goodrum-Abreu-Rushton House

THORNTON-JONES HOUSE
Architect,
Philip Trammell Shutze, 1936
West Paces Ferry Road, Buckhead

PHILIP SHUTZE (1890–1982) rarely wrote about his architecture, but in the year he completed this house for Albert E. Thornton, Jr. (1885–1953), and Mrs. Thornton, Edna Hill McCandless (1890–1978), Shutze expressed his classical credo for an Atlanta architectural journal, *The Southern Architectural Review.* Describing at length why he had chosen the classical revival style for the Temple on Peachtree Street instead of "anything ultra-modern,"

Shutze said: "This new modernism . . . has already begun to be a little shopworn and lacking in vitality. To try to be different is always fatal artistically: it seems more fitting to employ the old forms and try to import to them a new freshness and charm." For the Albert Thorntons, Philip Shutze gave some of the forms of late eighteenth- and early nineteenth-century English and American neoclassicism a fresh and charming interpretation: on the front, the Regency manner of the English architect Sir John Soane (1753–1837) and on the rear, the American Federal.

In so doing, Philip Shutze was neither unmodern nor un-American. He was of his own time, yet timeless. Fiske

Kimball (1885–1955), a pioneer scholar of American architecture, has shown so well that formal eclecticism and classical revivalism was the modern way for Americans in the late nineteenth and early twentieth centuries. In his *American Architecture* (1928), Kimball asked: "What is modern architecture?" He answered: "It affirms a principle of style that uses classic elements, to be sure, but is not merely imitative. It reaffirms the supremacy of form, and works in the classical spirit of unity, uniformity, and balance." Kimball said that the American classical revival leaders, such as Charles F. McKim (1847–1909) of McKim, Mead & White, "like men in other periods of reserved interest in unity and purity of form had turned to classicism's masses and spaces of geometrical simplicity—which offered an established language widely understood."

The Albert Thorntons chose one of the most fluent of the American classicists, one of the Deep South's best, and certainly Atlanta's most classically trained architect. A Columbus, Georgia, native and an exact contemporary of Mrs. Thornton's, Shutze had won the Rome Prize in 1915, which McKim established in 1894 at the American Academy in Rome, Italy.

Albert Thornton, Jr., was a grandson of General Alfred Austell, one of Atlanta's pioneer citizens. In 1865 Austell founded the Atlanta National Bank, which later became the First National Bank of Atlanta (First Atlanta). Thornton was a native Atlantan, a graduate of the University of Georgia, 1905, of Yale, 1906, and of Columbia Law, 1909. A financial and civic leader, he was also a much-loved social figure, president of the Piedmont Driving Club and of the Capital City Club. He was eulogized in 1953 by the *Atlanta Constitution*: "In building a successful career and in helping to build a great city, he had not neglected to build many lasting friendships."

His wife, Edna McCandless, was also an Atlanta native, but with deep roots in Wilkes County, Georgia; she was one of Atlanta's most respected cultural leaders. When the Georgia Fine Arts Committee was formed in the mid-1960s to create the Georgia Governor's Mansion, several blocks away on West Paces Ferry, Edna Thornton was chosen

chairwoman of furnishings; she expressed her standards in these words: "It's a question of quality and taste, not money!"

These were the standards she used in helping Phil Shutze give form to her own house and grounds, which reflect in many subtle ways the British character of the early architecture of Georgia. The stucco neoclassicism of Augusta and Savannah, much of it ultimately derived from the influence of Sir John Soane, is the background from which Shutze's design evolved. The rear or garden elevation is especially reminiscent of two landmark houses in Augusta, the Phinizy and the Kilpatrick; both of these early nineteenth-century Federal houses also feature one-story classical porticoes with curving double stairs.

The entrance façade is more purely Soanesque, displaying a one-story version of a typical Soane *bombé* motif, containing the curving entrance hall. The taut surfaces of this gate-lodge-like apse, in the Soane manner, have linearly grooved pilasters much like those at

Opposite: Entrance. Above: Entrance hall. Top: Garden elevation.

Soane's Pell Wall (1822), which has a two-story *bombé* garden front. Further underlining the Soanesque character of the Thornton façade are rows of dentil-like ball drops, which Shutze also uses to ornament the entrance hall. (Soane devised this personal classical detail to

use throughout his house, 13 Lincoln's Inn Fields, London, c. 1812, which was Soane's "experiment station" for his own delightful essays in creative classicism.)

The present owners, Frank and Annie Anderson Jones of Macon, Georgia, who purchased the house in 1978, maintain it much as Philip Shutze designed it. The estate is smaller in acreage now, but the immediate grounds and gardens still provide the perfect setting for the house as Shutze designed them, when this was one of the last great estates built along West Paces Ferry Road.

In Fiske Kimball's epilogue for his *American Architecture* of 1928, he wrote: "Among the American architects are more than one who gives promise of living on as masters who can speak out of the past in the eternal language of form." With this house, designed for one of Atlanta's builder families, Philip Shutze speaks to us in that classic yet not unmodern language that is still much loved in Atlanta.

Governor's Mansion
Architect, A. Thomas Bradbury & Associates, 1968
391 West Paces Ferry Road, Buckhead

ATLANTA BECAME THE CAPITAL of Georgia in 1868, succeeding Milledgeville, where the Executive Mansion was built in 1838, 130 years before the state built this new mansion in Atlanta to house its governors. The old mansion in Milledgeville, a classical revival house of exceptional quality, was "an acknowledged masterpiece," according to Professor John W. Linley in *The Architecture of Middle Georgia* (1972). For thirty years that mansion served the purpose for which it was designed, housing governors in style—eight in all. Now restored and open to the public, it is the President's Home of Georgia College.

Neo-Palladian in architecture, the old mansion was part of the Jeffersonian classical revival. Thomas Jefferson believed that the early American republic should express its aspirations with architecture reminiscent of the buildings of the ancient civilizations of Greece and Rome. Neoclassical architecture was the official style of the early American republic, and the old Georgia Governor's Mansion was a monument of that revival when it was still more Roman than Greek; still Jeffersonian and neo-Palladian.

With that fine precedent in mind, no one was surprised when in 1966 the State of Georgia decided to build a new classical revival house for its governors to replace the large granite bungalow on the Prado in Ansley Park. (House Resolution 235-694, authorizing the new mansion, described the house in Ansley Park, which had been the home of eleven governors, as: "cold, gray, austere, and medieval.")

The site of the neoclassical mansion on West Paces Ferry Road was part of a 25-acre estate, called Woodhaven, which belonged to the late distinguished banker and former Atlanta mayor, Robert Foster Maddox (1870–1965). Eighteen acres were purchased, including the formal terraced garden. A special Governor's Mansion

Opposite: Entrance elevation facing West Paces Ferry Road.
Above: Original terraced garden of the Robert Foster Maddox
estate, Woodhaven.

Committee of the Georgia General Assembly suggested the site and the style of the facility. An Atlanta architectural firm headed by A. Thomas Bradbury was chosen to design the building, P. D. Christian Company was the contractor, and Edward L. Daugherty was the landscape architect. Construction was begun in 1966 and the house was dedicated in January 1968.

Thirty fluted columns of the Doric order surround the rectangular brick body of the house, supporting an unornamented wooden cornice. These columns, 24-feet high and made of California redwood, rest on a porch floor paved with St. Joe brick laid in a herringbone pattern; there is no balustrade. The front entrance doorway is based on an Asher Benjamin design from the 1830s.

Decisions about gardens, grounds, and furnishings were made by a Fine Arts Committee of Georgia citizens. Coincidentally, the first resident of the new mansion was Lester G. Maddox, governor from 1967 to 1971. (He was not related to Robert Foster Maddox.)

The Fine Arts Committee assembled an outstanding nationally recognized collection of early nineteenth- century neoclassical antiques and art objects. For the most part the decorative arts are American-made, from the Federal period; c. 1825–1835, seems to be the cut-off date for inclusion.

The building's formal beauty and dignity is a great addition to West Paces Ferry Road. Many visitors and passersby think of it as the actual home of Georgia's governors since the antebellum period. (One clue that it is not an antebellum classical house is the absence of chimneys.) The 24,000-square foot mansion and the eighteen-acre estate along one of Atlanta's finest residential thoroughfares cost two million dollars. Today, that seems economical for a place of this scale, which must function as a family residence and as a mansion for state occasions.

Governor's Mansion

Right: State Reception Hall looking into drawing room (on the left) and circular stair hall, showing nineteenth-century giltwood chandelier. In the niche is a bronze bust of Benjamin Franklin, 1778, by French sculptor Jean Antoine Houdon. The roses on the c. 1800 podium table were grown and arranged by Elizabeth Harris, the wife of Governor Joe Frank Harris. Above: Drawing room.

Governor's Mansion

RICHARDSON-FRANKLIN HOUSE
Architect, Aymar Embury II, 1932
West Paces Ferry Road, Buckhead

IN THE 1830s, one hundred years before this house was built, Hardy Pace (1785–1864) established a ferry on the Chattahoochee River. The road from Pace's Ferry to the Buckhead crossroads, where Peachtree and Roswell roads intersect, is now called West Paces Ferry, and is one of the traditional centers of fashionable residential life in Atlanta. In May 1911, when the Tuxedo Park Company began selling a large tract of land west of the site of the present Governor's Mansion (1968), along and adjacent to the road, the *Atlanta Journal* called it "a splendid rolling tract in which cool woods and the fragrant scent of pines invite home-builders to tarry."

From West Paces Ferry Road north along the west side of Northside Drive toward Nancy Creek is a large estate that was developed in the early 1920s at the same time that the Tuxedo Park Company opened the area for residential development. Hugh Richardson, Sr., who himself dealt in real estate, purchased this land and in 1915 built a weekend cottage; his home then was on West Peachtree Street across from the Biltmore Hotel. He liked his country property so well—it was private and quiet—that in 1923–24 he built a large American Georgian Revival house called Broadlands. His architect, also a Princeton graduate, was Aymar Embury II (1880–1966) of New York. Embury

Top: Entrance elevation. Right: Norman keep, garden, and cobblestoned courtyard. Opposite: Entrance foyer looking toward courtyard.

was well known as a designer of American country houses; in 1909, for example, he published *One Hundred Country Houses.* Embury worked in the South frequently and some of his designs were included in *Southern Architecture Illustrated*, published at Atlanta in 1931.

‧ When that interesting book, filled with a number of Atlanta houses, was published, the home of Hugh Richardson's son, Hugh, Jr., in Brookwood Hills was included. Several years later Hugh, Jr., built this house on the West Paces Ferry end of his father's one-hundred-acre estate. In 1963 he moved to Broadlands, turning his house over to his daughter, Frances Richardson Howell, later Mrs. DeJongh Franklin, who still resides here.

The Richardson family estate has been large enough for several genera-

tions of relations to enjoy living near its meadows and streams—Wolf Creek, for example, crosses the property as it flows into Nancy Creek north of the Richardson-Franklin house, which stands at 900 feet elevation. Frances Franklin's portion of the spacious acreage, approximately eleven acres, has served her well in rearing her children and in her love of gardening. The house evokes Normandy with simple means; a Norman tower or keep is quite evocative of Norman architecture, as is the cobblestoned courtyard that the painted-brick house embraces. This enclosure provides Mrs. Franklin, as it did her mother before her, a walled garden at her dooryard. Old-fashioned Betty Prior roses, which tolerate the semishade, retain a hint of her mother's original pastel rose yard by the tower.

Richardson-Franklin House

Above: Stair hall looking toward living room. Right: Living room

Richardson-Franklin House

On a level elevation above Nancy Creek, on property adjacent to Hugh Richardson's Broadlands estate, Philip Trammell Shutze designed for Mr. and Mrs. Fred W. Patterson this sophisticated yellow-and-white farmhouse in the late 1930s. For the past twenty-five years it has been the home of Mr. and Mrs. Julian S. Carr.

An example of the early American vernacular in which Philip Shutze often worked after he designed Swan House for the Edward H. Inmans, the Patterson-Carr house is designed to seem to be an eighteenth-century house that has grown by a process of addition and become more sophisticated through the years. Although built all at once, the whole seems to be made up of parts that have been beautifully assembled and composed. It has personality inside and out, and, though informal, is not decorated as if it were a working farmhouse. (It is early American, but decidedly not the work of a bumpkin.) It is of the very essence of the revival of early American architecture that Stanford White and others originated around 1900, and the Atlanta firm of Hentz, Reid & Adler (and later Hentz, Adler & Shutze) began to investigate in their own Colonial Revival designs.

The classical Vitruvian principles have been realized within a simplified American Georgian format: useful

*Left: Entrance elevation facing
Northside Drive. Above: Entrance from
motor court.*

space, well-built structure, and delight-ful effects to please the user and the observer. One effect is the way the house is conceived as part of the land-scape, an element in the total composi-tion. This is an indoors-outdoors kind of house with a garden vista or garden access for each principal room. To cre-ate the sense of a bower within the house, there is an Athos Menaboni dog-wood mural in the L-shaped main hall. To heighten this effect, the hall opens

into an enclosed garden. (Anne Coppedge Carr is a respected gardener and garden historian, active in the Gar-den Club of America.)

With the Patterson-Carr house, Philip Shutze practically defined the Anglo-American concept of a house that is one's *home*: "a dwelling-place, abode; the fixed residence of a family or household; the seat of a domestic life and interests." (Oxford University Press, 1901)

This is how the Atlanta, Georgia, house and the Atlanta, Georgia, home probably ought to look; especially when the dogwood and Japanese cherry trees planted down the entrance lane are showing spring col-ors; when the white-rail fence and pickets and the yellow-and-white clap-boards are warming in the sun; and when the deep green mounded box-wood is pungent by the arched and shuttered entrance door. This is subur-

153

ban Atlanta at its best. As H. Stafford Bryant of the Classical America Society wrote in 1977: "Atlanta did not have the first, or even the largest of the great leafy suburbs, with each dwelling in its own large park, but in northwest Atlanta may well be the culmination of the entire movement."

The Patterson-Carr house is a distinct contributor to that culmination: an American suburban house that has the

ambience of the rural countryside and of a house that is not brand new, but antique; yet at the same time has all of the latest conveniences, is only fifteen minutes from two major shopping malls, and twenty minutes from the financial district.

Fully equipped with modern domestic amenities, this house fulfills every requirement of a dwelling in the twentieth century, yet has the

Above: Living room.

manners and refinement of several generations of good architectural breeding. Philip Shutze of Hentz, Adler & Shutze captured this classic Atlanta Spirit in domestic architecture for the Fred Pattersons in the 1930s, and the Julian Carrs have appreciated, preserved, and further refined it into the 1990s.

Above: Hall with Athos Menaboni mural.
Below: Dining room.

Patterson-Carr House

MARTIN HOUSE
Architect, James Means, 1965
Fairfield Road, Buckhead

THE BROADLANDS ESTATE extended north from West Paces Ferry Road along Northside Drive toward Nancy Creek and into the area where this house was built in 1965 just above the south bank of the creek. It is a country house in a suburban setting.

Peggy Sheffield (Martin) rode horseback over these fields and meadows when she was growing up and this area was considered far more "country" than it is today. (The illusion of a country house is still sustained by the great sweep of meadowland and the creek, an eighteenth-century English-landscape setting for the architecture. Heightening this bucolic impression is a wooden bridge spanning Nancy Creek, a old landmark on the bridle paths through the woods and fields.)

Louise Richardson Allen, who grew up at Broadlands, reminisced in 1988 about a Buckhead of a different era: "In 1927, a group of our neighbors organized what was called the Saddle and Sirloin Riding Club, and they used to meet on Saturday mornings." One of those neighbors was Mrs. Robert White, from whom the Martin's purchased their property and whose house still graces Fairfield Road.

After Peggy Sheffield's marriage to Thomas E. Martin, Jr., she and her husband created—on this former riding turf—a serene, beautifully sited home—perhaps the most handsome of all the houses by James Means

Opposite: Entrance elevation.
Above: Stair hall.

Martin House

(1904–1979). Inside and out, Means evoked for them the James River plantations of Tidewater Virginia, which both the Martins remembered from their days at Virginia colleges.

To say that their place is perhaps Means's masterpiece is saying something, as a glance through the book about his works would reveal. Each of some fifty handcrafted houses was not only eighteenth-century in style and detail, but eighteenth-century in spirit. In *The Houses of James Means (1979)*, Mrs. John Ray Efird wrote: "James Means was possibly the last living architect trained in the 18th-century manner, before the schooling of architects became institutionalized and codified. He learned as Christopher Wren's generation did—from apprenticeship to

master designers and from the original books. All designs by James Means were purely Means, but have fooled experts who guessed them to be genuine 18th-century buildings."

The domestic scale and classical proportions that Means learned to draw during his apprenticeship with Hentz, Reid & Adler and continuing with Hentz, Adler & Shutze was matched by an exceptional scholarly knowledge of period ornament and craft skills. One of the first to work for Neel Reid, Means was one of the last to work for Philip Shutze, helping Shutze until the firm went out of business in 1951 and Means went out on his own.

Jimmy Means's career was unusual for his day, when an academic education for architects had become stan-

dard. Starting as an office boy for Reid in 1917 when Means was fourteen, he worked part-time at first, and then began to go to the office more and more to learn—in time becoming one of the firm's best draftsmen and assistants. After graduation from high school, he enrolled in architecture at Georgia Tech, but soon, by choice, was back full-time at Neel Reid's side, learning from a master until Reid died in 1926. During those years Means began to work with Philip Shutze, whose education was more formal and academic. After Shutze settled into the firm and became a partner in 1927, Means and Shutze worked together daily until Shutze retired. It was a large office, with many talented men. Jimmy Means was never a registered architect, but he

helped produce the best houses built in Georgia in his day.

Means was well-known for his love of old houses and authentic, old building materials. He used salvaged materials, but only if they came from buildings past saving. He knew craftsmen and contractors who could do what he needed, but there were few of them left.

Jimmy Means did not begin working entirely alone until 1954; he and Edward Vason Jones, another Georgia classicist, had worked together for several years after Philip Shutze retired, but no one working exclusively in Georgia had Means's unique lifetime knowledge of the classical architectural tradition—learned directly from Reid and Shutze and kept alive in his own

Opposite: Living room.
Top: Dining room. Above: Den.

work. His daughter, Mary Catherine Means, a professional preservationist, wrote in the book about her father's work: "James Means continued to produce uniquely elegant classical homes until quite recently, yet he was relatively unknown beyond his circle of clients and staunch admirers. As more scholarly attention is paid to the undercurrent of classicism in twentieth-century architecture, James Means may yet achieve national recognition."

Peggy Sheffield Martin is still one of his staunchest client-admirers. All designs by James Means were "purely Means," but one almost has to rub one's eyes. Is that Carter's Grove or Westover across that meadow? No, it is the subtle melding of the two in the architectural alchemy of James Means.

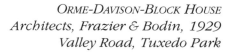

ORME-DAVISON-BLOCK HOUSE
Architects, Frazier & Bodin, 1929
Valley Road, Tuxedo Park

SINCE 1929 THIS HOUSE has had only a handful of owners, a rarity in fast-changing Atlanta. The present and immediately preceding owners are of the same family: Margaret Davison Block and Bates Block, daughter and son-in-law of Dr. and Mrs. Thomas Callahan Davison, moved into the house in 1957 soon after their marriage. Dr. and Mrs. Davison had purchased the property in 1943, and when they removed some undergrowth and trees, newly revealing the house to Valley Road, many people thought they had just built it. Dr. Davison, an outstanding surgeon, was chief of staff at Georgia Baptist Hospital.

Aquilla J. Orme, a lawyer, president of the Atlanta Title Company, and real estate developer, and for whom Orme Circle is named, was the first owner. The house was built by Charles H. Black, Jr., the son of Tuxedo Park developer Charles H. Black, for whom Blackland Road is named. The partnership of Daniel H. Bodin (1895–1963) and Charles E. Frazier (1889–1939) produced this and over a dozen more of the major houses in the Blacks' elegant suburb. Margaret Davison and Edward Bates Block (1918–1990) had been married only a few months when this became their home, which it had already been for the bride since she was a child.

The furnishings are a mixture of Davison and Block heirlooms, some crafted especially for their families, including a handsome breakfront made for Mrs. Block's mother by an expert Atlanta cabinetmaker, the noted Jens I. Krogh.

The Blocks have also employed the special talents of their nephews when making improvements to the house and grounds. Traditionalist designer G. Kenneth Garcia, Jr., designed the Palladian cabinet in the solarium for Mrs. Block's remarkable porcelain collection, the arched cabinet that balances the doorway into the living room, and the newly completed entrance steps. Landscape architect

Brooks Garcia recently replanted the entrance area to compliment the Georgian Revival façade.

Margaret Block, a member of the Cherokee Garden Club, loves "the grounds, the yard, garden, and pine trees," as she has from the days when her parents first moved here during the era of World War II. From the original larger acreage, Mrs. Block now has two and one-half acres to manage, and she does the work with style and the help of an experienced gardener. Her garden features elements from notable nineteenth- and early twentieth-century Atlanta gardens, including some exceptional cast-iron lawn furniture from Bates Block's grandfather's house that

stood in the 1890s on Peachtree Street at Ponce de Leon Avenue. A contemporary iron garden gate crafted by Ivan Bailey further emphasizes the fact that these Atlantans have combined a sentimental appreciation for the heirlooms from their family history with a confidence in their own tastes. The special place that Margaret and Bates Block have created is a charming and obviously loving embodiment of the Atlanta Spirit at home.

Opposite: Front elevation from Valley Road. Left: Entrance stair ball. Above: Living room, looking into solarium.

Orme-Davison-Block House

Above: Dining room. Below left: Breakfront by Atlanta cabinetmaker Jens I. Krogh. Below right: Solarium, with cabinet designed by Kenneth Garcia, Jr. Opposite: Garden.

Orme-Davison-Block House

Top: Entrance elevation.
Above: Entrance hall.

NO OTHER ARCHITECTS were considered when the Efirds decided to build on nearly seven heavily wooded acres on a hill in Tuxedo Park above Wolf Creek. It was the sort of building site dear to the heart of James Means (1904–1979), a dedicated and uncompromising artist whose services Callie Huger Efird admired well enough to wait for more than a year to obtain. Meanwhile the site—from the street about a quarter of a mile through the hilly woods—was cleared and the winding driveway built while she awaited the busy architect. Old materials, a Means trademark, were gathered: one-hundred-year-old bricks salvaged from a downtown Atlanta warehouse, heart-pine random-width

flooring, and seasoned pine for paneled walls.

She and the architect chose as inspiration for the design, the graceful, unpretentious architectural vernacular of early eighteenth-century Virginia and Maryland. West St. Mary's Manor, a small story-and-a-half Maryland landmark of early-American classicism, provided basic ideas in plan, form, and detail. Philip Shutze had encouraged James Means's native abilities and taught him to be a complete designer, with a perfectionist's undeviating interest in every detail, including fabrication, inside and out. Just as Neel Reid had before them, Shutze and Means included interior decoration and landscape garden design within the archi-

Stair hall looking into living room. The design of this stairway was based on that at West St. Mary's Manor, c. 1700-1730, in southern Maryland. Note the wide heart-pine floor boards and stair treads.

Efird House

Above: Living room. The paneled fireplace wall is in the style of the early eighteenth century, while the "tray" ceiling above the modillion cornice lends height and dignity. Below: Living room looking into entrance-stair hall.

Above: Dining room off the central hall, with paneled fireplace wall and antique fireplace tiles. Below: Informal dining room at the rear of the house, with wide heart-pine paneling. The Federal period Southern pine corner cabinet holds an excellent collection of blue-and-white Chinese export porcelain.

tect's purview. They were of the old school, which intended to create harmoniously convincing original designs within the spirit of chosen historical periods and styles.

Callie Huger Efird was editor of *The Houses of James Means*, published in June 1979 as an outgrowth of a planned Means house tour benefit that never took place because of Means's tragic death in an automobile accident in February of that year. The book is "a lasting and loving tribute" by Means's client-friends, as Callie Efird wrote, who "appreciate the lasting contribution he made to our lives by the houses he designed." The Efirds' house, dating from 1965, well

represents some fifty houses carefully selected for that book, all within the state of Georgia, the majority in metropolitan Atlanta. Each was a solid work of conservative, precedent-inspired domestic architecture, which twentieth-century Atlantans have preferred and commissioned with success, even as traditionalist architecture became more and more of an anachronism nationally.

Mrs. Efird's furnishings, a museum-quality assemblage of antiques and fine art, complete the gracious scene set by James Means's learned and exacting but creative essay in the classicism of the early eighteenth-century upper South.

Efird House

BLACK HOUSE
Architect, Clement Johnston Ford, 1985
Valley Road, Tuxedo Park

TUXEDO PARK has been called "the Camelot of Atlanta's residential areas with picture book mansions, rolling green acreages and wooded backdrops." This was in of an article in the "Intown Extra" section of the *Atlanta Journal-Constitution*, September 29, 1988; the staff writer Actor Cordell continued in a different tone: "But it is in danger of losing its character from the breakup of large estates into subdivisions, and some homeowners are complaining." This newspaper story addressed the development of cul-de-sac subdivisions, carving up the neighborhood piecemeal, with whole new streets running off the old ones and a half-dozen or more new houses on quarter-acre lots adjacent to existing residences.

The Dameron Black house, however, does not represent the usually unfortunate trend that has led to legal fights over proposed historic-district zoning and other types of restrictions. Bitter controversies, pitting neighbor against neighbor, have often been about small points of interpretation rather than larger issues of protecting quality of life and aesthetic integrity. Rather than being controversial, the

Dameron Black house is a representative of the best of what can be done within an established context. The home of Dameron III and Jane Swann Cocke Black continues a classic Atlanta tradition within Tuxedo Park, begun in the earliest days of the neighborhood's development.

The Black home is one of around six hundred within approximately two square miles, bordered by West Paces Ferry on the south, Randall Mill Road on the west, Blackland Road and/or Nancy Creek on the north, and Powers Ferry and Roswell roads and Andrews Drive on the east. The Tuxedo Park Company of 1911, and later the Valley Road Company, were real estate enterprises of Charles H. Black and his son Charles, Jr., an expert building contractor. By 1930 the present configurations of the Park were in place. The grandest street is possibly Valley Road, especially the southernmost portion where this house is located. At this point it is a broad avenue that parallels Wolf Creek before it becomes a winding stream cutting through hillier terrain. Here are some of the largest mansions, with drives curving off through spacious green lawns and naturalistically landscaped lots; much of the forest is old and stately, and generally the land is 850 to 950 feet in elevation.

The Dameron Blacks built their house in 1984–85 on a portion of the fourteen-acre estate of Jane Black's parents, Frances Floyd and the late Emory L. Cocke, who built here in 1930 their

American-Georgian Revival home designed by Will Griffin. (Mrs. Cocke's father, James Swann Floyd, was an early investor in Tuxedo Park real estate.) In 1982 the Blacks chose Clement J. "Clem" Ford (b. 1906) as their architect.

They showed him a layout with a good many suggestions from Jane Black's mother, and Clem Ford did some initial working drawings. After studying the blueprints, the Blacks and their architect decided on a final design that very

Opposite top: Entrance elevation.
Opposite bottom: Detail of entrance hall through living room doors.
Above: Entrance-stair hall.

Black House

*Left: Living room facing garden. Above: Garden elevation,
classical revival, Regency in character.*

much pleased them all. In August 1985 they moved in. David Byers, an Atlanta-based interior decorator classicist, helped Jane Black in the early stages of the work, advising her and the architect toward readying the house for the Blacks' move.

Their house is one of Clem Ford's last designs; he retired soon afterward due to the effects of a stroke. One of the last of the Atlanta traditionalists, he was graduated in architecture from Georgia Tech in 1928 and Columbia University in 1930. In New York City in 1930 and 1931 he worked first for Dwight James Baum and then for William Lawrence Bottomley, two of America's best house designers. Ford returned to Atlanta in 1931 to specialize in residences, clubs, and schools, and similar domestic-scaled buildings. Among his works were renovations to the John W. Grant home on West Paces Ferry for its conversion to the Cherokee Club in 1957, and major additions and alterations to the Piedmont Driving Club in 1963. Clem Ford's sympathetic classicism is sorely needed as Atlanta grows and as new buildings are added to older neighborhoods—some of them among America's most beautiful and prestigious garden suburbs, such as Tuxedo Park.

Left: Dining room looking into solarium. Top: Solarium-breakfast room.
Above: Solarium-bar looking toward living room.

Black House

HOWELL-McDOWELL HOUSE
Architect Albert Howell, 1932
Peachtree Battle Avenue, Buckhead

MRS. MICHAEL McDOWELL said in an interview for *Landmark Homes of Georgia* in 1982, "This was Pop's dream house; Albert fell for Italy." The widow of the late Albert Howell (1904–1974), Caro du Bignon Henry Howell McDowell, has continued to live in her first husband's dream project since he completed it for her in 1932—a young architect's home for himself and his bride. The Howells married in 1930 and took a five-month wedding trip to romantic, out-of-the-way places, returned to Atlanta, and lived in an apartment while this house was being built. It stands on an elevation surrounded by gardens on land originally acquired by Judge Clark Howell

(1811–1882), Albert Howell's great-great-grandfather, who had operated a sawmill and gristmill on the creek nearby. Albert's share consisted of seven acres. (His great-grandfather, Evan Park Howell [1839–1905], owner of the *Atlanta Constitution*, hired Henry W. Grady, champion of the New South creed. The *Constitution* under Evan and his son Clark [1863–1936] glorified the South's past while urging acceptance of the present to create a brighter future—the Atlanta Spirit.)

This scion of Atlanta's prominent Howell clan was one of the first native

Left and above: Entrance elevation.

*Above: Stair hall looking into dining room. Below: Octagonal entrance
hall decorated with paintings by Athos Menaboni.*

Atlantans to study architecture; he followed a not unusual route at the time, attending the schools of architecture at the Georgia Institute of Technology and Columbia University, and spending a period of time at the École des Beaux-Arts in Paris. He met his bride-to-be in Paris where she was residing with her mother. That they should be introduced was perhaps natural, as they were both from old, well-known Georgia families, although Caro du Bignon Henry did not grow up in the home state of her ancestors. The du Bignons were originally French royalists, coming to Georgia in the late eighteenth century and purchasing Jekyll Island as their plantation. (In

1886 John Eugene du Bignon sold the island to a group of northern millionaires and socialites. With them he formed the Jekyll Island Club, a fabled organization once headed by J. P. Morgan.)

Albert Howell practiced architecture, beginning in 1929, with McKendree A. "Mac" Tucker. A small Italian villa that the firm designed for Mrs. Hunter Cooper on Andrews Drive in Atlanta, in the beginning of their practice, is similar to Howell's own home, but because it may be seen from the street, it is better known than his dream house. Included in *Southern Architecture Illustrated* (1931), Mrs. Hunter Cooper's house shows how

Above: Parlor looking into entrance hall.
Below: Library with glimpse of garden pavilion.

well the Italian idiom can be adapted to suit a suburban Atlanta landscape, especially when the color of the stucco matches the sienna tones of Atlanta's soil. Tucker & Howell were also included in Philip Johnson and Henry Russell Hitchcock's catalogue on modernistic architecture published by the Museum of Modern Art, *The International Style 1922–1932*. Their entry in that famous exhibition was decidedly not an Italian villa but a small, functionalist science museum in the mountains of Highlands, North Carolina.

The early 1930s were transitional, with the Beaux-Arts aesthetic yielding to the new Germanic Bauhaus approach. (Harold Bush-Brown, who was head of the development of architecture at Georgia Tech during the time Albert Howell studied there, has written about the period in his *Beaux-Arts to Bauhaus and Beyond* [1976]). Even though to survive as architects in those Depression days, Tucker & Howell sometimes designed in the style of International modernism, Albert's heart was in the traditionalism and classicism of his villa on Peachtree Battle Avenue.

Howell based his home on the front of a small villa by Andrea Palladio in Montecchio, Italy, Farni-Cerato, 1542. The house, not visible from the busy street just below, is sited atop a hill that slopes dramatically away on all sides. The rear of the house opens onto a ter-

Howell-McDowell House

race, which looks out on a lawn and a balustrade, before the land descends in terraces down to a classical garden pavilion. The hidden terraces are used for growing flowers and vegetables. The garden elevation was inspired by a villa in Guy Lowell's *More Small Italian Villas and Farmhouse* (1920), a book in Albert Howell's library. The house has the scale and proportions of a pavilion, as the French call a villa-sized house set in a garden.

Adorning the façade above and flanking the entrance are panels with reclining figures by the late Atlanta sculptor, Julian Hoke Harris. The main entry from the tranquil exterior of cool stucco and lush hydrangeas leads into an equally serene octagonal room with four panels of Italian countryside views by Athos Menaboni (1895–1990). These panels were painted on site for the house when Menaboni first came to Atlanta; he was a native of Livorno, Italy, and became world famous for his paintings of native birds and other wildlife. Howell based the design of this marble floor on the Empire bathroom, Palazzo Pitti, Florence, Italy, 1811–12.

The stair hall is decorated with arabesques and birds of paradise painted by Paul Chelkco and Harvey Smith;

Smith helped the Howells with interior decoration for many years. The design of the dining room mantelpiece was inspired by a fireplace in the Villa dei Collazzi built in the early sixteenth century in Tuscany.

At Albert Howell's death in 1974, his conception was more than forty years old. As it nears sixty years, Howell's Palladian Revival dream villa grows more classic. It would not be unlike what a young architect today might attempt if he were of the new school of classicists and eclectics, sometimes called postmodern. Albert Howell would probably approve of any trend toward classicism, even one as idiosyncratic as postmodernism. As an illustration of what he thought about the highly personal architecture of Frank Lloyd Wright (1867–1959), America's native modernist, Mr. Howell commented to this writer in 1956, "Wrong!" he answered characteristically with a pun, "Frank Lloyd Wrong."

The Atlanta Spirit in domestic architecture has been and remains revivalistic and generally conservative. The Palladian villa of Atlanta native Albert Howell well embodies that spirit, and is still occupied by people who love it and give it life.

HOWELL HOUSE
Architect, Henri V. Jova, 1976
Arden Road, Buckhead

ON THE HILL above and adjacent to the Albert Howell property is the home of Fay and Barrett Howell. Mr. Howell, who is a great-great-grandson of Judge Clark Howell, has said that his grandfather, Clark Howell (1863–1936), publisher of the *Atlanta Constitution*, ". . . was probably the first Howell to have permanent residence in the Buckhead area, and that was at the turn of the century. He had a country house [on the site] and there weren't many other people out here."

During the Civil War, just before the Battle of Peachtree Creek, July 20, 1864, Barrett Howell's great-grandfather, Captain Evan Park Howell, C.S.A. (1839–1905), commanded a battery of artillery in this immediate vicinity. Captain Howell, opposing Federal General J. W. Geary's division as it moved south across Howell's own land toward the City of Atlanta, is said to have shelled the very spot from which Bar-

rett Howell now surveys the city that his family helped rebuild after the war.

From this site, where the Clark Howell house had stood, Barrett Howell is able to observe how effectively this work of city building has been achieved. He does so from a house that combines classical and modern, the old and the new, designed by one of the city's most talented architects, the ever-youthful Henri Jova, FAIA.

A native of New York State, Henri Jova, whose name suggests his French and Spanish origins, came to Atlanta in the 1950s after an exceptional preparation for his architectural career at Cornell, a Rome Prize fellowship in 1950 from the American Academy in Rome, and a Fulbright fellowship in 1951. His cousin, the Atlanta architect Francis L. Abreu, was his first employer and one of his first landlords; Jova lived in a guest house at the Abreu home on West Paces Ferry, now the Southern Center for International Studies, which another Rome Prize fellow, Philip Shutze, had designed.

Henri Jova is the senior designer and a founding principal partner of Jova/Daniels/Busby. He is one of the acknowledged leaders in the redevelopment and restoration of Midtown Atlanta, where he has resided since 1958 in an intriguing and urbane family complex. Paralleling his architectural and interior design interests is his painting, in many media, especially of imaginative architectural subjects.

Opposite top: Entrance hyphen, containing the hall and dining room, connects the living area of the house to the master suite and kitchen area. Opposite bottom: Southern elevation. Above: Meadow. Below: Entrance hall with view of the distant skyline.

Howell House

Jova's is a colorful style that combines abstractions and representation, not unlike his architecture. His firm no longer designs residences, which makes those that he did even more appreciated. Of another of his designs from the mid-1970s, Jova has said: "It's a contemporary house that responds to a collection of antique furnishings of quality."

The home of Barrett and Fay Sheffield Howell does this also, at the same time that it responds to the extraordinarily historic and visually appealing setting. The dramatically scaled sitting room, the entrance hall, and the library all embrace the wooded piedmont plateau site and the city skyline beyond in such a way that they become an element in the interior design.

Similarly, the Howells' collections have become part of the architecture, especially in the sitting room and in the library, which quietly blends the old and the new, a disciplined contemporary eclecticism rooted in Jova's classicism. Atlantans pride themselves on their spirit of conservative respect for the old, unhindered by a narrow parochialism that would prevent fresh solutions to old problems.

Far left: Sitting room. Above left: Sitting room view of the piedmont setting and modern Atlanta. Left: Sitting room. The north wall of the room was designed to accommodate the Howell porcelain collection.

Howell House

Left: Dining room. Top: Library.
Above: Entrance and stair hall.

ON A SEVEN-ACRE, heavily forested lot, well known for its woodland garden of native azaleas, this picturesque English Tudor-style house nestles just off Peachtree Battle Avenue. The Peachtree Heights Park neighborhood is an elegant subdivision dating from just before World War I, designed by the New York architects Carrére & Hastings. It has remained among the most beautiful in north Atlanta, with a neighborhood association that proclaims its determination in its name, Peachtree Battle Alliance.

Built for Mr. and Mrs. Leon Baker, this has been the home of Comer Legare Jennings for nearly thirty years. Jennings is originally of Eufaula, Alabama, where the Comers, his mother's family, are well-known and numerous. One was Alabama Governor Braxton Bragg Comer. Jenning's father was president of Cowikee Mills, a family business with a number of mills in south Alabama. The interests and talents of Comer Jennings, however, turned him toward writing and drawing instead of textiles. After time

in the Navy, Emory University, and Princeton, he returned to Emory to graduate. Advertising was his first job, in Philadelphia, then New York, where he became an account executive and married Ann May of Burlington, North Carolina, with whom he had two sons. He continued in advertising when they moved to Atlanta in the early 1960s to raise their family. *Atlanta* magazine, October 1965, described Comer Jennings as "one of a new professional breed who have given polish to the advertising world in Atlanta." Through all of this he had kept up his painting and drawing, painting "about four nights a week." In New York he had studied at the Art Students League and in Atlanta at the Atlanta Art Association's school. His paintings began to win awards, and people started commissioning portraits. At home he converted a garage into a studio.

By the late 1960s he had retired from advertising to become a professional painter, his avocation becoming his vocation, and in 1968 he added a

studio at the rear of his house. His artist's eye called for the addition to blend with the original Tudor style, which he and his architect W. Caldwell Smith achieved in association with designer Otto Zenke, who also planned the interior decoration.

Comer Jennings is best known, perhaps, for portraits; among those who have sat for him are former President Jimmy Carter, Robert W. Woodruff, and Ambassador Philip Alston, Jr. His vibrantly colored still lifes are also much appreciated, and he is not timid about trying his hands at something new.

The artist Comer Jennings, now a bachelor, has become so much a contributing part of the cultural life of Atlanta that his spirit has become a vital part of the classic spirit of Atlanta.

Above: Entrance elevation facing Woodward Way. Opposite top: Living room. Opposite far right: Entrance detail. Opposite near right: Entrance hall from living room.

187

Above: Patio with view of studio. Below: Den. Opposite: Studio.

Jennings House

HENTZ-LANE-MORRISON HOUSE
Architects, Hentz, Adler & Shutze, 1936
Muscogee Road, Peachtree Heights Park

IN ATLANTA it is rare to be able to list with only three surnames the history of the ownership of a house. The provenance of an item of the decorative and fine arts is an important part of its value and interest—"from the collection of" in an auction catalogue is often as interesting as who fashioned the object. The same can apply to a work of domestic architecture, and this is especially significant when the original owner was also its architect, or at least was an architect who built it for himself as his home. The first surname in the provenance of this house, Hentz, is also that of the architectural firm listed as responsible for its design. The second name, Lane, purchased the property as Hentz was retiring from his architectural practice

in the late 1940s and preparing to move to his native state of Florida; and the third name, that of the present owner, Morrison, a nephew of the Lanes, was added in 1973. As with the Tompkins house, the architect's design intentions have been understood and preserved; the only significant addition to the property occurred in 1949 when the swimming pool on the west side of the bedroom wing of the house, one of the first private swimming pools built in Atlanta, was added by the Mills Bee Lanes.

Hal Fitzgerald Hentz (1883–1972) was born in City Point, Florida, May 15, 1883, and died in Winter Haven, Florida, February 16, 1972. Graduating in 1904 from Emory College, when it was still located at Oxford, Georgia,

east of Atlanta, Hentz commenced his architectural education—along with Neel Reid, who became his architectural partner—by taking a year, 1907–08, at the École des Beaux-Arts in Paris. He completed his formal architectural work at Columbia University in 1912. Four years later he married Frances Connally, younger daughter of Dr. Elijah Lewis Connally of the Homestead, West End, and a granddaughter of Georgia's antebellum governor and then New South leader Joseph E. Brown. The Hentzes had no children, and Mrs. Hentz died in 1941. Her obituary in the *Atlanta Constitution,* January 11, 1941, reported: "The home and garden of Mr. and Mrs. Hentz are among the famous ones in Atlanta."

Opposite: Entrance elevation facing Muscogee Road.
Above: Parterre garden.

At the time this house was built, Hal Hentz was the senior partner of the most prominent architectural firm in Atlanta. He and Neel Reid had formed their partnership in 1909, adding Rudolph Adler, a construction specialist, in 1916 to create Hentz, Reid & Adler, and, in 1927, the year after Reid's death, the name Shutze was added to the letterhead, which then read: "Hentz, Adler & Shutze, successors to Hentz, Reid & Adler, Candler Building, Atlanta, Hal F. Hentz, R. S. Adler, Phil Shutze."

The house was featured in *Southern Architectural Review*, June 1937, in this way: "Hentz, Adler & Shutze Design a Residence for a Member of the Firm." This title and the wording of the text settle any question about whether Hal Hentz alone was the designer: "The work of the firm has been admired for many years, and it is now of great interest to observe the application of the principle on which they have worked to the residence of the senior member of the firm." The article continued: "The situation and design of a Greek Revival house on an irregular and romantic plot presents difficulties seldom so happily solved. Few trees have been cut down and a relatively small amount of grading done. The effect was secured largely through the judicious situation of the building in regard to the street and to the garden." One of the principles for which the firm was known was especially well represented here: "The plan and mass arrangement of the garden as well as the planting of the house itself were designed by the architects."

The Howard J. Morrisons have in their house-history file an original pen-and-ink sketch, washed with color, of the east side of the property, with the garden parterres in the foreground and the east elevation of the house in the background. This beautiful unsigned sketch is in the style of Philip Shutze, the firm's chief designer, who must have been the member of the firm most responsible for the successful outcome of the difficult design problem.

The interior reflects the exterior formality and symmetry, but with an easy graciousness that relates to the informality and natural beauty of the wooded site. The plan is organized around a central hall that leads directly into a din-

Top: View from living room into entrance hall. Above: Entrance hall looking into dining room. Above right: Living room, with view of parterre garden.

ing room with a curved wall of windows—a bay, Regency in character, that provides views of dogwood trees and other hardwoods to the rear of the lot. Inside and outside are so thoughtfully related that no room is without a leafy view or a glimpse of a terrace or a gar-

den spot embowered in trees.

This rolling wooded terrain is a beautiful aspect of the architectural character of Peachtree Heights Park, which was carefully planned before World War I by the New York architects Carrére & Hastings for the E.

Rivers Realty Company. Many of the houses in the neighborhood were designed by Mr. Hentz's firm, and none is more successful than this twentieth-century evocation of antebellum Georgia's one and one-half-story Greek Revival cottages. A design complete inside and out, it is traditional but contemporary, the firm's ideal.

The Hentz-Lane-Morrison house seems only to grow more classic and beautiful as it ages, becoming more of a work of art whose provenance of only three loving owners has helped to protect it from heedless adulteration. It *is* a lovable embodiment of that gracious manner wherein the Old South and the New, the traditional and the contemporary, meld into a style we call the Atlanta Spirit.

Hentz-Lane-Morrison House

"The Barclay" was a model home designed in 1930 by Lewis Crook for Herbert Kaiser (1891–1985), developer of Lenox Park, and built in 1931. The first owner and resident was Fred Houser; today it is the home of the Barbara and Dale Rays, college professors who have reared their family here. Moving to Atlanta in 1966 from Ann Arbor, Michigan, for Dr. Dale Ray to teach electrical engineering at Georgia Tech, they had instantly liked the Morningside-Druid Hills in-town suburban area. Barbara Ray is also a college professor, of Urban Studies, at Georgia State University, having earned her doctorate since moving from Ann Arbor. The Rays loved the trees surrounding their house and the garden suburb layout of

the neighborhood. They have loved, too, the plan of the house—the way it "lives and breathes;" Crook designed it for the hot, humid summer weather of Atlanta before the days of air conditioning.

The Rays are the fifth owners since the model was built as a demonstration for the Lenox Park developers, Land Lot Three Realty Company, of which Herbert Kaiser's father was owner and Kaiser, the CEO. In the company's advertisements "a handsome modified English-type one-story was designated as 'The Barclay.'" Additionally they offered "The Chateau" and "The Sussex," also designed by Crook and supervised by his partner, Ernest Ivey.

"The Barclay" was included in *Southern Architecture Illustrated* (1931) as the Fred Houser residence. Its "modified English," or simplified Tudor, style of dark red brick and several gables toward the street, did indeed help set the pace in the neighborhood.

The original Lenox Park tract consisted of 150 acres of piedmont woodland, northeast of Ansley Park, divided into some three hundred sizeable lots. It began at East Rock Springs on the south and went from Pelham Road on the west to Lenox Road on the east. Considerable space was given to wide streets, sidewalks, and parkways. These characteristics have been preserved. At major entrances into the subdivision were classical brick piers topped with elegant limestone urns; some of these monuments had disappeared, but in 1990 the Morningside-Lenox Park Civic Association began erecting a series of nineteen exact replicas according to Lewis Crook's original design.

Lenox Park is on the eastern end of Morningside and is usually considered part of it. Morningside was developed beginning in 1923 by James R. Smith and M. S. Rankin of Morningside Park. It was annexed to the city in 1925, and Lenox Park followed in 1931. The earliest settlement in the area was known as Easton, a farming community centered at Walker's Gin and Grist Mill on Clear Creek near where it flows beneath Piedmont Road north of Piedmont Park. In 1934 just north of there, Smith Park was built at the corner of Piedmont and Monroe Drive to honor Morningside developer, the late James R. Smith. In the center of Smith Park in 1990 the civic association erected one of the commemorative classical piers with this legend, "Morningside-Lenox Park, 1923."

Morningside-Lenox is a vibrant and beautiful garden suburb of distinctive homes, churches, and schools, only minutes from the business districts of downtown, Midtown, Virginia-Highlands, and Emory University-Druid Hills. "The Barclay" was a model home for Lenox Park, and so it remains, in the capable, appreciative hands of professors Dale and Barbara Ray.

Above: Entrance elevation.
Opposite top: Living room.
Right: Study.

Ray House, "The Barclay"

DANIEL BERRY FRANKLIN is an Atlanta native from families of many generations of residency in this city and its environs. A University of Georgia economics major in the middle of a business career, he decided to return to his alma mater in Athens to study landscape architecture in Professor Hubert Bond Owens's renowned program. Franklin's landscape architecture degree was awarded at the twenty-fifth reunion of his original college class.

Franklin maintains a studio with

Above: Entrance elevation. Opposite: Living room looking toward dining room and "Privy Garden."

apprentices at his home on Cottage Lane in Collier Hills just as he had in Ansley Park where his late mother, Zulette Crumley Franklin (1881–1962), and late brother, James A. Franklin, Jr., had lived for many years. Dan Franklin's Ansley Park garden was also a showcase of his great garden-design and green-thumb talents.

His Cottage Lane garden has been called the "Privy Garden" (*Gardens of Georgia* [1989]), as in belonging to a person in his individual rather than his official capacity; private; secret. This is the landscape architect's private garden, his own creation behind his house, for himself and his guests, rather than for a client. Dan Franklin's

characteristic sense of fun is also at work in the name, which is a pun—a private joke; Dan calls his summerhouse the "Franklin Outhouse," just as he had in Ansley Park.

Collier Hills lies along either side of Collier Road on lands originally settled by Andrew J. Collier (1827–1887), a pioneer resident of Fulton County who operated a gristmill on Tanyard Branch before the Civil War. In July 1864 the Battle of Peachtree Creek raged here along the stream valley, which was a strategic location for the Federal forces as they headed south toward town. Now Collier Hills is a peaceful suburban neighborhood, desirable because of its traditional cot-

tages, modest in size but stylish, and the rolling wooded setting, much of it in park land. The neighborhood was planned and built in the years just before and after World War II by the well-known Atlanta contracting firm of Herbert W. Nicholes (1871–1959) and his son Martin (1892–1982), that built fine houses in Druid Hills and all around the northern suburbs of Atlanta. Dan Franklin bought his Nicholes-built c. 1940 cottage at Christmas 1979.

Cottage Lane sits on a ridge running north off Collier Road toward the Bobby Jones Golf Course just above Tanyard Branch. It is appropriate that Dan should live on ground made historic during the Civil War. The diary of his grandmother, Mrs. William C. Crumley, Caroline "Carrie" Berry (1854–1921), daughter of pioneer Atlantan Maxwell Rufus Berry (1803–1909), is one of the prime references for Atlanta during General W. T. Sherman's siege in the summer of 1864. Carrie Berry was nine years old when she made her first entry in her siege diary: "Gen. Johnston fell back across the river on July 19, 1864, and up to the time we have had but few quiet days. We can hear the cannon and muskets very plain, but the shells we dread." The Maxwell Berry house, where she vividly recorded many of these Civil War events, stood at the corner of Walton and Fairlie streets, the absolute center of old downtown Atlanta just west of Five Points. Carrie wrote: "A shell has busted under the dining room which frightened us very much. One passed through the smokehouse and a piece hit the top of the house . . . but . . . none of us were hurt. We stay close in the cellar when they are shelling." On August 3, 1864, she wrote: "This was my birthday. I was ten years old, but I did not have a cake, times are too hard so I celebrated with ironing. I hope by the next birthday we will have peace in our land so I can have a nice dinner."

That is the spirit out of which Atlantans like Dan Franklin have come.

In April 1987 *Southern Living* featured Dan Franklin's house and garden. The article began: "Ask Dan Franklin for an opinion, and you're sure to get one. Especially about gardening. If ever a person loved and understood gardens, it's Dan." The article continued: "His is not a big garden at all; it's a small one, set in a suburban Atlanta neighborhood. You need only step inside the house to catch the view." Dan planned the garden as an extension of the house even before moving in. "He pushed out the back wall of the house, enlarging the dining room and kitchen, and enclosed it in glass." As *Southern Living* reported: "This visual connection makes the garden a pleasure from indoors or out. The house and garden function as one, thanks to the wall of glass and a terrace that serves as an outdoor living room."

Daniel Berry Franklin's cottage pavilion set in the Collier Hills woods, and oriented toward his "Privy Garden," is a personal twentieth-century interpretation of a whole spectrum of earlier garden types, both formal and informal, eighteenth and nineteenth century. A demonstration of his professional acumen, this peaceful garden spot is what his Georgia ancestors hoped for when the bombs were "bursting in air" above these hills during the siege and battles more than a century and a quarter ago.

"Privy Garden" with summerhouse.

Franklin Cottage

THE CHATTAHOOCHEE RISES in mountainous north Georgia, passes by the village of Vinings and the outskirts of the city of Atlanta, as it flows to Columbus and on to the Gulf of Mexico. "Out of the hills of Habersham, Down through the valleys of Hall," rhapsodized Sidney Lanier, Georgia's favorite native-son poet in his often-memorized poem, "Song of the Chattahoochee" (1877).

Rebel Ridge rests above this gentle river, which was the approximate dividing line of two nations of native Americans, the Cherokee to the north and east, and the Creek to the south and west. The Indian village of Standing Peachtree, where Peachtree Creek joins the river, and Fort Peachtree, built in 1814 on the east bank at the same juncture, were here before Hardy Pace (1785–1864) operated a ferry in the area and, in the late 1830s, became one of the first white men to settle legally across the Chattahoochee in the land formerly a part of the Cherokee Nation.

After Andrew Jackson passed through the territory in 1820 on his way to Alabama, he wrote about "white intruders north of the Chatahoochey [*sic*]." East of the river, DeKalb County was created in 1822 and then settlement began to be authorized where this house stands in what is now Fulton County.

North of the site of Fort Peachtree and south of Paces Ferry Road as it crosses the river toward Vinings, Beverly and Frances DuBose built their home and settled in 1951. At that time they were themselves practically pioneers, so far out from Buckhead and downtown Atlanta was their wooded riverside site, and so little other construction then existed on either side of the river.

Frances Woodruff DuBose was from Columbus, Georgia, which is often called Columbus-on-the-Chattahoochee, so she felt right at home by the river in far suburban northwest Atlanta. This was natural ground too for the late Beverly Means DuBose, Jr.

(1918–1986), a Civil War expert and the nation's preeminent private collector of Civil War· artifacts. In the immediate area of their house, both Federal and Confederate troops were encamped in the summer of 1864. From his living room, Beverly DuBose could see Vinings Mountain, from which General William T. Sherman first viewed Atlanta in 1864, as the general headed south

from northwest Georgia.

The house at Rebel Ridge was designed for the DuBoses by a talented firm of classicists begun by Henry J. Toombs (1896–1967), a native of Cuthbert, Georgia. Toombs had worked for McKim, Mead & White in New York City after graduating in architecture from the University of Pennsylvania and study abroad. He was Franklin D. Roosevelt's architect for buildings at Hyde Park, New York, and at Warm Springs, Georgia: the Little White House, 1932, and classical revival buildings for the Warm Springs Foundation, some as late as 1966. (Appropriately Henry Toombs was a great-nephew of Georgia's "Unreconstructed Rebel," Robert Toombs.) The project architect for the DuBose house was Warner Morgan.

The DuBose's Rebel Ridge is a seventy-acre tract. Cannons stand at

Opposite: Entrance elevation. Above: Living room. This room originally ended at pocket doors that opened onto a balcony for ventilation and the charm of the river below.

DuBose House

the driveway on the site of a Confederate battery that guarded the Paces Ferry crossing. As a young man, DuBose developed an interest in Civil War artifacts, sharing his father's fascination with the Atlanta battlefields. Beverly M. DuBose, Sr. (1886–1953), was born at Sewanee, Tennessee, where his father, a veteran of the Confederate army, was an administrator at the University of the South. Beverly, Sr., became a student of Civil War history, although he never had a passion for collecting artifacts. While his father studied military strategy, young Beverly searched the fields for *minié* balls.

His senior thesis at Emory University, where he graduated *cum laude* in 1939 with a degree in history, covered the Atlanta campaign.

Several years after he was discharged from the Navy, he bought war surplus mine detectors and used his knowledge of the trenches and campsites in and around Atlanta and throughout most of the Civil War battle zones to uncover great quantities of guns, bayonets, bullets, cannonballs, shells, sabers, and swords. In 1953 he and his son Beverly "Bo" M. DuBose III dug out a space under their house and built a room to hold

the constantly growing collection.

At his death there were six display rooms for the collection: uniforms, canteens, saddles, flags, paintings and prints, and pieces of furniture, in addition to the weapons and munitions, all displayed in staggering array. Much of the material he had collected personally, but some came from dealers, other collectors, and inheritors. Artifacts—as well as the very site of his home—brought the war to life for Beverly DuBose; he was especially interested in the people who fought and died for what he once described as a principle: "The

Left: Dining room. The Chattahoochee River, flowing past Rebel Ridge, is visible from the dining room bay.
Above: Display room. This is only a portion of the largest private collection of Civil War artifacts in existence, destined for display at the Atlanta Historical Society.

right to live in a chosen manner."

Although DuBose was a lifelong "Rebel," and he specialized in things Southern, his extraordinary collection of war artifacts came from soldiers of both sides. Before his death he gave his collection for permanent display at a new facility of the Atlanta Historical Society, where his father and he had served as president, and he as chairman for the last seven years of his life. A great contributor to the Atlanta Spirit, Beverly DuBose lives on through the magnificent collection he loved and labored to create throughout an Atlanta lifetime.

ON A WOODED SITE with a little stream in the north Atlanta suburbs is a modern plain-style classical house, the home of Georgiana collectors who have specialized in what they have called "neat pieces"—the plain-style furniture of nineteenth-century Georgia. (See *Neat Pieces*, Atlanta Historical Society, [1983].) Not all of their furnishings are, strictly speaking, plain. But all are antiques: American, Southern, and Georgian, with a few British things—perhaps as a reminder that, after all, Georgian derives from the state's English heritage.

The Griffins bought the land in 1958, before the metropolis had spread very far into north Fulton County. Their preliminary plans for the site were drawn by Mr. Griffin's uncle, Will, the talented classically trained architect for whom he was named, but who had moved away from Atlanta by the time the Griffins were truly ready to build. They asked their architect-friend Tom Collum, who was then working for the firm of Stevens & Wilkinson, to begin thinking about the design. It was the first house Collum designed on his own.

Top: Entrance. Opposite: Living room looking through entrance hall into dining room. Above: Living room with view of balcony.

Griffin House

Above: Family room. Opposite top: Guest bedroom. Opposite bottom: Terrace.

Stevens & Wilkinson had been the first Atlanta architectural firm to work in the modernist idiom. In the late 1930s its Bauhaus-influenced International Style pavilion (now demolished) for Judge Price Gilbert might have signaled a landmark change in Atlanta's domestic design, if anyone had followed suit. Collum's design for the Griffins is in a vernacular-Georgia-modern idiom, a modern classicism stripped down to the essentials, much like some of their Georgia-made furniture they call plain style. The architectural references take form in simplified classical pediments and dentils.

This is a contemporary classicism, expressing the love the Griffins feel for the simplicity of Atlanta's early nineteenth-century piedmont plateau beginnings, when plantation-plain-style houses were built in the countryside around the railroad terminus. A preserved example of this kind of yeoman farmer's dwelling is the Tullie Smith House, now a museum at the Atlanta Historical Society and a favorite restoration project with which the Griffins were closely associated in the 1970s. Florence Griffin was one who helped make the grounds and gardens of the restoration, especially the plant materials, authentic to the Georgia piedmont in the 1830s and

1840s. Her horticultural knack and knowledge show at home.

Together Bill and Florence Griffin have become experts on the material cultural heritage of their native state. Their house, with its superb collections of furnishings, is a landmark of the Atlanta Spirit, because it is an artistic interpretation of the city's background in the Southern countryside. For more than a century Georgians and other Southerners have been coming to Atlanta seeking to enjoy the advantages of the capital city of the state and of the New South. Atlanta has always had both its plain and its fancy sides; this is the classic best of the "plain."

207

SMITH HOUSE, BELLMERE
Architect, Jack R. Wilson, 1986
North Fulton County

ON THE NORTH, where Fulton County extends into the foothills of the Blue Ridge, there are still unspoiled acres near the Chattahoochee River that attract those who would escape the more settled suburbs nearer town. Bellmere is located northwest of the Chattahoochee near the Fulton-Forsyth-Gwinnett county lines, a 325-acre estate far from a main highway. Overlooking a small lake, the house and garden are deep within the wooded property, which the Smiths treat as an arboretum. Deen Day Smith, a former president of The Garden Club of Georgia, and Charles O. Smith, Jr., are both native Georgians with a traditional love of the land. Bell Road shows on early maps of north Fulton County and *mere* is a thirteenth-century Middle English word for lake or pond, as well as for landmark: thus Bellmere, a landmark house of Atlanta's far northernmost Fulton County suburbs. (In England Bellmere would be considered a country house.)

Fulton, the home county of the city of Atlanta, is the most heavily populated of the eighteen counties in the Atlanta Metropolitan Statistical Area. Named for Robert Fulton, the county was created in 1853 out of DeKalb County. In 1932 Campbell County was annexed on the south and Milton County on the north. The result is sixty-two miles long, from the northeast, near Alpharetta, the county seat of old Milton County, to the southwest near Campbellton, the county seat of old Campbell County. The resulting shape is somewhat like an hourglass, leaning to the right or east, with Atlanta

as the sand suspended in the middle.

A unifying feature of the county from one end to the other is the Chattahoochee River as it flows from northeast, near Bellmere, in a southwestern course toward the meeting of the Fulton County line with Carroll and Coweta counties, near the riverside site of old Campbellton. Near Roswell the river becomes the western boundary of the county for much of its course in the area. On the northeast, the river forms the county line between Fulton and Gwinnett, from near Bellmere on the far northeastern corner until the river turns and crosses the county at its narrowest point just south of Roswell—the point where the "sand" falls through at the "waist" of the hourglass shape.

Atlanta, therefore, and the county of which it is the governmental seat, have developed a linear pattern of settlement from south Fulton—through downtown, Midtown, and Buckhead within the city limits—to the northern suburbs along Interstates 75 and 85 and Georgia Highway 400. Much of what we call Atlanta is within the home county, but much more, in fact, continues to spread out into DeKalb, Cobb, Cherokee, Forsyth,

and Gwinnett, and other counties, many on the south, within one of the fastest-growing metropolitan areas in the United States—the twelfth largest in 1990.

The growth of these Atlanta suburbs has spawned hundreds of thousands of houses, but few are as fine as Bellmere in continuing the classic Atlanta tradition—twenty-five miles from Buckhead. The Smiths' architect, Jack Wilson, a classicist from Moultrie, Georgia, first visited the site with a civil engineer in a "four-wheel-drive jeep" to site the house on the estate. The lake was not yet built. He and the engineer chose the best building spot, which Wilson says, "was the only place to put it." He designed the entire plan, including the positioning of various outbuildings, in 1983 and early 1984, and the Smiths moved in by 1986. A major consideration of Deen Day Smith's was the function of the plan for entertaining. The solarium overlooking the rear walled garden needed to be large enough to accommodate one hundred guests at a seated dinner.

Jack Wilson says that the style of the house is American classical, a revival house without over-studied and specific references and precedents; an estate in the "big house" tradition of an earlier day. Jim Gibbs of Atlanta laid out, planted, and largely maintains the grounds and gardens, for which he has received a national landscaping award. Virginia White, a longtime associate of Mrs. Smith's, helped her with all aspects of interior decoration, including acquisition of decorative arts of exceptional quality.

Opposite: Entrance elevation. Above: Living room looking through entrance hall into dining room.
Below: Entrance-stair hall.

209 *Bellmere*

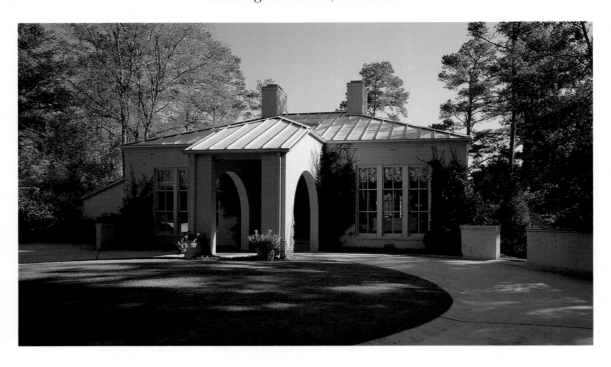

GEORGIAN REVIVAL domestic architecture, which is sometimes called Anglo-Palladian, has been first in the hearts and minds of Atlantans since the days of Neel Reid and his associates. Edward Inman II's family, for example, is closely identified with the Anglo-Palladian Swan House, now part of the historical society's Atlanta History Center. His and his wife Suzanne Barnes Inman's home, however, is no conventional 1980s developer's "Georgian traditional," with lots of what newspaper ads sometimes call "Palladium [*sic*] windows." Charles W. Moore (b. 1925), their distinguished architect, said in a June 1985 interview published in the "Home and Garden" section of the *Atlanta Journal-Constitution* soon after the house was completed: "The owners and I sat around talking about the style of the house. I think we decided it was sort of turned-on Georgian. It's not postmodern."

Nevertheless, Charles Moore's work has had a major influence on postmodern architecture. Moore, an architect, author, and teacher, was the 1990 recipient of the gold medal of the American Institute of Architects. In announcing the institute's highest award, the *New York Times*, December 18, 1990, reported that Moore is known

for "whimsical buildings that integrate historical styles." One of his best known designs is the Piazza d' Italia in New Orleans, which is a decidedly festive statement of columned classicism. Paul Goldberger, the *New York Times* architecture critic, says that Moore's work "represents the highest aims of postmodernism, standing as proof that history is neither to be feared nor to be embraced simplistically."

Moore stated in 1985, "My architecture is distinguished by the quality of space inside, the way things line up and some of the nice oversized elements." He is known for personal, often playful, interpretations of classicism and has been called "a grandfather of postmodernism."

Formerly the dean of architecture at Yale University, Moore has also taught at the University of California at Berkeley and Los Angeles, as well as at Princeton and Harvard. In 1991 he is a professor of architecture at the University of Texas at Austin.

The Inmans' place is off Randall Mill Road, which runs north of West Paces Ferry Road, adjacent to Tuxedo Park on part of the rear garden of an older house. They and the architect have produced a house designed as a

harmonious unit with its grounds and gardens; thus, it might be called the Inman villa, a postmodern classical villa for a young couple in the 1980s.

Moore's co-authorship of *The Poetics of Gardens* (1988) should be noted. In this fascinating book, he examines gardens from the past, in various climates, to understand basic principles and traditions that can be applied to the creation of new American gardens. Moore was already well-known for that point of view as it applies to architecture, as he has demonstrated here.

The Inmans collaborated with Moore and their landscape architect, Atlantan Daniel B. Franklin, in the final design to coordinate the house and garden into a formal statement, Anglo-Palladian in feeling, but with few, if any, exterior ornamental details of obvious Georgian derivation. The bedroom wing terminates in a courtyard-pavilion-porch, Moore's version of a classical loggia integrating the inside with the outside in the Palladian manner.

Charles Moore's skill in designing homes, whether for the Inmans in Atlanta or for others, literally in the far reaches of the world, was expressed best by the architect himself in a

September 1990 interview in *Architectural Digest*: "The culmination of the experience of a work of architecture should be finding a place where you feel comfortable, where you can sit down after journeying a hundred miles or a thousand miles and feel as though you're there, that you've arrived at the center of the world."

The center of Edward and Suzanne Inman's world is in the harmonious symmetry and geometry of their beige-pink painted-brick villa—a fresh tribute to Andrea Palladio's Renaissance classicism. Moore's "turned-on Georgian" is a classic Atlanta villa for the late twen-

tieth century, a rejuvenation of the Atlanta Spirit in architecture in its long love of the Georgian period.

Opposite: Entrance elevation. Above: Bedroom wing and courtyard-pavilion-porch.

Opposite: Entrance hall looking out to courtyard and pavilion.
Above: Living room, with view through hall to dining room.

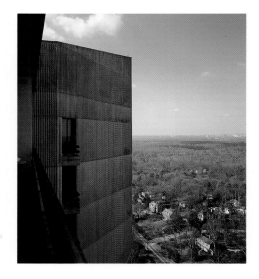

PEACHTREE STREET becomes Peachtree Road at Brookwood Hills, where Palisades Road meets Atlanta's best-known thoroughfare. Peachtree had been a stylish residential address for single-family dwellings from the 1890s until the 1920s, but as garden suburbs were built on either side of the ridge, shops, stores, businesses, apartments, churches, and other institutions began to dominate the streetscape. This process continued apace until it quickened in the 1950s and 1960s, even in Buckhead along Peachtree Road.

In the early 1970s, near the church towers at the intersection of West Wes-

ley, East Wesley, and Andrews Drive, the first high-rise apartment-condominium complex in the Buckhead area was built. Designed by Ted Levy, Plaza Towers provided a standard of contemporary luxury for high-rise homes, with spectacular views over the treetops of north Atlanta and south toward a downtown business skyline rising higher by the month.

Today, just north of Plaza Towers across Peachtree Road, stands the tallest and most massive of all the residential towers, Park Place, also by Levy. William and Mary Scott Rooker purchased the condominium space that

Ted Levy had reserved for himself at the top of the building he designed. The Rookers also purchased adjacent space to pull together five thousand square feet of living area.

As at Plaza Towers, residents of Park Place fashion their interiors individually to suit their needs and tastes, within the structure of a modernistic envelope. The Rookers had lived for fifteen years in Cobb County on a large acreage at the Chattahoochee River. Their house had been designed by Jimmy Means, one of Atlanta's best classicists at midcentury. To design their Peachtree penthouse in a domes-

tic-scaled classical mode comfortable with Ted Levy's modernism, they chose the youthful Atlanta architect, Norman Davenport Askins. Askins, a native of Mountain Brook, Alabama, is one of the best classicist architects now practicing in Atlanta, and he is helping breathe fresh life into the classical tradition for this generation. A graduate in

---

Opposite top: Park Place towers over the traditional homes of Buckhead.
Opposite bottom: Balcony off dining room overlooking West Wesley Road.
Above: Entrance hall.

architecture at Georgia Tech and of the masters program in architectural history at the University of Virginia, Norman Askins has a wide-ranging knowledge of the fundamentals of classical design and creates original designs within the tradition.

Work on the Rooker penthouse began in January 1989 and was completed in the fall of that year. Askins, the Rookers, and the interior decorator, Dottie Travis of Atlanta, decided on an early nineteenth-century style and ornamentation, reminiscent of William Jay's Richardson-Owens-Thomas House (1819) in Savannah, itself an interpretation of Sir John Soane's Regency. The restrained and reductive classicism of the Regency period complements the planar geometry of Levy's Park Place exterior.

Askins's boldest statement in the Rookers' penthouse is found within the spacious proportions of the dining room, where great faceted columns and a delicately vaulted ceiling create a theatrical space overlooking the leafy terrain of Buckhead far below and the north Georgia Appalachian chain on the horizon.

Dottie Travis also helped Mary Scott Rooker with details of interior decoration, using many heirlooms that Mrs. Rooker's mother is sharing with her appreciative daughter. The well-known Greensboro, North Carolina, interior decorator, Otto Zenke, was the source of many of the antiques that now adorn the Rookers' penthouse.

In the last decade of the twentieth century, therefore, the Atlanta Spirit takes form in great new commercial spires and *stadia* of Olympian grandeur and begins to reside in homes above the clouds. Interestingly and predictably, however, even within the modern framework of the Park Place tower, that very same spirit still finds comfort and expression in the classical taste of William and Mary Scott Rooker's penthouse home.

Dining room.

WHEN ANDREW YOUNG CAMPAIGNED IN 1981 for the office of mayor he promised to make Atlanta an "international city." The campaign rhetoric of the former United Nations ambassador was nothing new for Atlanta. Rather than proposing something avant-garde, the ambassador was speaking the classic language of the realm.

Andy Young was a new generation appealing to the most traditional heart and soul of the city's great old booster tradition dating back to its earliest days. A uniquely prideful sense of civic destiny is the Atlanta Spirit. Centered at Atlanta after the Civil War, the Bourbon Democrats devised the formula. Atlanta should not only be the new capital of Georgia but the capital of a New South. When Bourbon-leader, governor and former Confederate general, John Brown Gordon dedicated the present Capitol, July 4, 1889, he declared, "In the fashion of its architecture [Renaissance Classicism], in the symmetry of its proportions . . . this proud structure will stand through the coming centuries as a fit memorial of the indomitable will and recuperative energies of this great people." Combining the legendary ideals of urbanity, gentility, and hospitality of the Old South with the urbanization, commercialism, and economic development of the Yankee North, Atlanta would be the gateway city for the post-War South.

Henry W. Grady was the chief spokesman and booster articulating this creed in his and the Howells' *Atlanta Constitution*, in speeches, and in national columns. In 1889 Grady wrote in the *New York Ledger*: "Dear to the new South . . . is the message of the old regime, its traditions and history." But, additionally, he made it clear, Atlanta would be the coming place in the Deep South, in which capitalism and development were welcome, as in Chicago and New York. That was to be the new kind of Southern hospitality, and Atlanta would be its home.

Northern newspaperman Whitelaw Reid commented in 1866 in his *After the War*: "The people of Atlanta were infected with the mania of city building." Not just New Yorkers saw this; so did fellow Georgians, as expressed in the Savannah proverb: "Atlanta has the nerve of a government mule. If it could suck as hard as it can blow, it could bring the ocean to it and become a seaport." When Milledgeville, the antebellum state capital, was about to lose its status to

Atlanta, the editor of a Milledgeville newspaper complained in 1867: "Our friends in Atlanta are fast people. . . . To a stranger the whole city seems to be running on wheels, and all the inhabitants continually blowing off steam." Teaching school in Atlanta, Miss Elizabeth Sterchi wrote home to Pennsylvania in 1868: "They speak of Berlin, Paris, London. Atlanta can very soon beat them; it is a little New York. . . . Like a polyp it extends its arms in every direction."

Andrew Young's expansive, seemingly new sense of the city's destiny, which he broadcast as he ran for the office that he won, was clearly the very essence of the place he wanted to lead; his was another step along the well-trod path toward full realization of the inland city's traditional mania with becoming a "seaport"—an "international city"—extending "its arms in every direction."

In 1905 Robert Foster Maddox, who became mayor in 1909, gave the rhetoric of the Atlanta Spirit tangible form at the start of the twentieth century. In a stirring, evangelical speech that Maddox made when he was president of the Atlanta Chamber of Commerce, he said:

"The 'Atlanta Spirit' was conceived in the time of Terminus, born in Marthasville, suffered under the fire of Sherman but rose again from the ashes of war to lead us with its white light through the dark days of reconstruction, and has since illumined the way for a brave and generous people, with ready hands and willing hearts to build a great city. . . ."

In 1908, U. B. Phillips, a leading historian of Southern history, and a native of LaGrange, Georgia, wrote: "The unabashed ambition of the people for their town, and their clamor of self-advertisement hastened her growth." In 1922 John R. Hornady commented in his *Atlanta, Yesterday, Today, and Tomorrow*: "The average Atlantan will not be satisfied until the city becomes one of the world's greatest centers of population . . . and is never quite so happy as when telling someone of its greatness."

It is probably no coincidence that Coca-Cola, never a shy company about advertisement, and long an international product, was developed in Atlanta. In 1950 Charles Howard Candler, son of Asa Candler—the founding Coca-Cola genius and, like Maddox and Young, an Atlanta mayor—wrote about his father:

Atlanta has the nerve of a government mule. If it could suck as hard as it can blow, it could bring the ocean to it and became a seaport.

SAVANNAH PROVERB

"During his administration as Mayor of Atlanta as well as before and after it, his own business experience with advertising led him to speak out strongly on the subject of 'boosting' the city. He was always active and helpful in the creation and maintenance of what was called the 'Atlanta Spirit.'"

Candler, also a Coca-Cola president, whose house, Callanwolde, is included in this volume, continued:

"My father's enterprise, wealth, and influence were always on call to back his almost sentimental conviction that Atlanta was destined for greatness among the cities of America. Speaking to the Chamber of Commerce several years before his election to the mayoralty, he had urged an advertising and publicity program for the city and said, 'The dawn of a greater Atlanta is at hand, the spirit of influence of which will spread across a horizon as yet undreamed of.'"

That the Candlers, and later Robert Woodruff, encouraged "the world to sing" about Coca-Cola should not be discounted in understanding the sanguine style of the city. In somewhat the same mold as Henry Grady, John Temple Graves, an Atlanta orator and newspaper editor (the *Atlanta Georgian*) wrote in 1943: "Whether they came from Coca-Cola or gave to it, the animations of Atlanta are like none other in these United States."

Mayor Andrew Young's internationalist aspiration for the city was in step with a long and honorable tradition, as was his post-mayoral work (with Billy Payne's Citizens' Committee, Mayor Maynard Jackson, and others) to blend the city's classic Phoenix-flame with the Olympic flame and hold it aloft for the world to see at the XXVIth Olympiad in the summer of 1996. In the life's blood of the city has been the realization of such seemingly impossible dreams.

Yet Andrew Young often billed himself as a non-traditionalist, as one who was building a "new kind of city." In 1986 as mayor he said, "We're building the city's character now," and he coined a catchy rhyme to refer to the city's historic landmarks—"hunks of junk." One landmark to which he especially applied the jingle was one of Atlanta's favorite late-Victorian monuments, "The Castle," sometimes called Fort Peace (opposite), an Ansley Park residence at Fifteenth and Peachtree streets, long converted to artists' studios. In the midst of the not altogether bad-humored debate, the rhyme became a rallying cry for local historic preservationists who fashioned a button, "Save Our Hunks of Junk," and in time they won some major points in the debate. (The Castle is preserved and restored as part of the A T & T Promenade, a twelve-acre office-hotel-retail complex.) The preservationists brought to his honor's attention a line of thought that he eventually seemed to accept in principle, that there are benefits for quality of life in preserving aspects of earlier periods of growth as living parts of the cultural environment. Preservation as a necessary form of progress in a truly international city became their theme. In 1988 a historic preservation steering committee announced the preparation of a comprehensive preservation plan for the city; later an ordinance was passed listing 109 sites and 49 landmarks.

Perhaps most vocal in opposition to the mayor's original position were the neighborhood civic associations. These community associations have been unusually successful at preserving one of the city's finest, most admired cultural resources—a splendid collection of planned garden suburbs, among them Inman Park, Ansley Park, Druid Hills, Brookwood Hills, and Tuxedo Park, many of them districts on the National Register of Historic Places, graced with handsome houses, gardens, shade trees and parks, churches, schools, colleges, and libraries.

Preservationists posed a fundamental problem. Is it possible to promote and create a city that represents "a grand type of progress, up to the most advanced ideas," as one of Henry Grady's mentors, I. W. Avery, wrote in 1885, and yet remains a place that has a liveable, human scale? If the spirit of the place is seemingly to be in a perpetual state of flux, how can already standing landmarks have a part in "progress" and be preserved? Can there not be older landmarks of the Atlanta Spirit among the new ones being created? Can these not contribute to an ongoing tradition of phenomenal urban, suburban, and exurban growth, reminding us of past triumphs and amenities? Can new Atlanta be as attractive a place to live as old Savannah—already a "seaport"—where historic preservation is practically a way of life, as opposed to Atlanta where historic preservation—given our "mania for city-building"—might seem antithetical and perhaps not a primary matter of public policy?

While the Atlanta skyline spreads north along Peachtree Ridge and beyond and changes with the ripple of each new economic muscle, many of the older well-planned residential neighborhoods within the city limits have not only survived the phenomenal growth, but have been improved and praised throughout the United States. The eager Atlanta Spirit of energetic progress ironically has produced handsome, stable, tree-shaded neighborhoods, and this optimistic dynamism and the gentle stability are recognized as being classic Atlanta. The consensus seems to be: Atlanta is a great place to work and to do business, yet a great place to settle down—to live in—to educate and rear a family. The city that the Bourbon Democrats started building after the Civil War, with the hospitality and urbanity of the Old South and the wealth and urbanization of the New, seems at hand.

In the long tradition of the boosterism that has been such a major part of the city's heritage, on February 5, 1989, the *Atlanta Journal-Constitution* put it simply and squarely in words that harken back to Henry Grady's New South formula: "Many who move to Atlanta for their jobs fall in love with the city. Maybe it's the quality of life, that mixture of old-time Southern gentility with the energy of modern growing Atlanta." Let us hope this familiar rhetoric, dear to Atlanta's heart, can still be used when the Metropolitan Statistical Area has reached ever new horizons, and new millions of people are MSA census statistics.

Let us trust that the story of Atlanta, rather than going, as some have predicted, from terminus to hubris to termination (from metropolis to imperial megalopolis to necropolis), always remains true to the old motto of the classic Atlanta Spirit—*Resurgens* (rising again)—like the Phoenix, on the city seal since 1887.

SELECTED BIBLIOGRAPHY

The fundamental source of information was Atlanta itself—the houses, gardens, parks, buildings and neighborhoods, terrain and topography. The author is an Atlanta native; his lifetime acquaintance with the city has produced a valuable personal archive of the place: newspaper and magazine clippings, brochures, leaflets, booklets, old books and magazines, old maps, prints, postcards, and photographs. Similar resources at the Atlanta Historical Society and the Emory University Woodruff Library were also essential. Books, articles, and research reports about Atlanta subjects written by the author are listed below. Information about houses and gardens and neighborhoods, which the author obtained by interviews between 1988 and 1991, was a primary source; home owners whom he interviewed are listed in the acknowledgments.

PUBLISHED MATERIALS: BOOKS

Allen, Ivan, Sr. *Atlanta From the Ashes.* Atlanta: Ruralist Press, 1929.

_____. *The Atlanta Spirit: Altitude and Attitude.* Atlanta: Privately printed, 1948.

Art Work of Atlanta, in Nine Parts. Chicago: Gravure Illustration Company, 1903.

Atlanta Homes. Atlanta: Presbyterian Publishing Company, 1900.

Avery, Isaac W. *Atlanta in the Empire State of the South.* Atlanta: Constitution Publishers Company, 1885.

_____. *The History of the State of Georgia from 1850 to 1881.* New York, 1881.

Bartley, Numan V. *The Creation of Modern Georgia.* Athens: The University of Georgia Press, 1983.

Bing, Sir Rudolf. *Memoirs, 5000 Nights at the Opera.* New York: Popular Library, 1972.

Black, Charles H., ed. *Tuxedo Park Company.* Atlanta: Privately printed, 1931.

Candler, Charles Howard. *Asa Griggs Candler.* Atlanta: Emory University, 1950.

Carter, Carol, ed. *Celebrating 150 Years of Atlanta Business.* Atlanta: Atlanta Business Chronicle and Atlanta Historical Society, 1987.

Central Atlanta Progress, Inc., ed. *Central Area Study II.* Atlanta, 1988.

Clarke, E. Y. *Atlanta Illustrated.* 2nd edition. Atlanta: Dodson & Scott, Printers, 1881.

Coleman, Kenneth and Charles Stephen Gurr, eds. *Dictionary of Georgia Biography.* Athens: The University of Georgia Press, 1983.

Crimmins, Timothy J. and Dana F. White. *Urban Structure, Atlanta.* Atlanta Historical Society, 1982.

Crook, Lewis Edmund, Jr., Foreword to *Southern Architecture Illustrated.* Atlanta: Harmon Publishing Company, 1931.

Cumming, Emily W. *Maxwell Rufus Berry's Family History.* Atlanta: Conger Printing Company, 1980.

Davis, Harold E. *Henry Grady's New South, Atlanta, A Brave & Beautiful City.* Tuscaloosa: The University of Alabama Press, 1990.

Downing, W. T. *Domestic Architecture.* Atlanta: Franklin Printing and Publishing Company, 1897.

Doyle, Don H. *New Men, New Cities, New South, 1860–1910.* Chapel Hill: The University of North Carolina Press, 1990.

Edge, Sarah Simms. *Joel Hurt and the Development of Atlanta.* Atlanta: Atlanta Historical Society, 1955.

Efird, Mrs. J. Ray, ed. *The Houses of James Means.* Atlanta, 1979.

Garrett, Franklin M. *Atlanta and Environs: A Chronicle of Its People and Events.* Reprint of the 1954 edition, I and II. Athens: University of Georgia Press, 1969.

_____. *Yesterday's Atlanta.* Miami: E. A. Seamann Publishing, Inc., 1974.

Griffin, William W., introduction. *Neat Pieces, The Plain-Style Furniture of 19th-Century Georgia.* Atlanta Historical Society, 1983.

Grady, James. *Architecture of Neel Reid in Georgia.* Athens: University of Georgia Press, 1973.

Gwin, Yolande. Introduction to *Atlanta at Home.* Atlanta: Egleston Hospital, 1979.

Henderson, Alexa Benson. *Atlanta Life Insurance Company.* Tuscaloosa: The University of Alabama Press, 1990.

Hewett, Mark Alan. *The Architect & the American Country House, 1890–1940.* New Haven: Yale University Press, 1990.

Hoehling, A. A. *Last Train from Atlanta.* New York: Thomas Yoseloff, 1958.

Hornady, John R. *Atlanta, Yesterday, Today, and Tomorrow.* American Cities Book Company, 1922.

Hunter, Floyd. *Community Power Succession, Atlanta's Policy-Makers Revisited.* Chapel Hill: The University of North Carolina Press, 1980.

Johnson, Willis, Jr., ed. *Peachtree Golf Club.* Atlanta: Stein Printing Company, 1978.

Kimball, Fiske. *American Architecture.* New York: Bobbs-Merrill, 1928.

Kurtz, Annie Pye. *Atlanta and the Old South, Paintings and Drawings by Wilbur G. Kurtz.*

Lane, Mills, ed. *The New South, Writings and Speeches of Henry Grady.* Savannah: Beehive Press, 1971.

Lyon, Elizabeth A. *Atlanta Architecture, The Victorian Heritage: 1837–1918.* Atlanta: Atlanta Historical Society, 1976.

Marsh, Kermit B., ed. *The American Institute of Architects Guide to Atlanta.* Atlanta, 1975.

Martin, Harold H. *Atlanta and Environs, 1940–1976.* Vol 3. Athens: The University of Georgia Press, 1987.

_____. *Three Strong Pillars, The Story of the Trust Company of Georgia.* Atlanta, 1974.

_____. *William Berry Hartsfield, Mayor of Atlanta.* Athens: The University of Georgia Press, 1978.

Martin, Thomas H. *Atlanta and Its Builders.* Atlanta, 1902.

Merritt, Carole. *Historic Black Resources Handbook.* Atlanta, 1984.

Miller, Paul W., ed. *Atlanta, Capital of the South.* New York: Oliver Durrell, Inc., 1949.

Mitchell, Margaret. *Gone with the Wind.* New York: The MacMillan Company, 1936.

Mitchell, William R., Jr., and Van Jones Martin. *Landmark Homes of Georgia, 1733–1983.* Savannah: Golden Coast Publishing Co., 1982.

Mitchell, William R., Jr. and Richard Moore, photographs. *Gardens of Georgia.* Atlanta: Peachtree Publishers, Ltd., 1989.

Mitchell, William R., Jr. *Lewis Edmund Crook, Jr., Architect.* Atlanta: The History Business, Inc., 1984.

_____. "Victorian Legacy, 1837–1905." In *From Plantation to Peachtree.* Atlanta: Southern Homes, 1987.

Mumford, Lewis. *The City in History.* New York: Harcourt, Brace & World, Inc., 1961.

Nesbitt, Robert, ed. *Inside Buckhead,* "Special 150th Anniversary Edition." Atlanta, 1988.

Parham, Louis L. *Pioneer Citizen's History of Atlanta, 1833–1902.* Atlanta, 1902.

Preston, Howard L. *Automobile Age Atlanta, 1900–1935.* Athens: The University of Georgia Press, 1979.

Rainwater, Hattie C., ed. *Garden History of Georgia.* Atlanta: The Peachtree Garden Club, 1933.

Ramsey, Stanley C. and J. D. M. Harvey. *Small Houses of the Late Georgian Period.* New York: William Helburn, Inc., 1923.

Richardson, A. E. and H. D. Eberlein. *The Smaller English Houses of the Later Renaissance, 1660–1830.* New York: William Helburn, Inc., 1925.

Russell, James Michael. *Atlanta, 1847–1890: City Building in the Old South and the New.* Baton Rouge: Louisiana State University, 1988.

Shavin, Norman. *Whatever Became of Atlanta?* Atlanta: Capricorn Corporation, 1984.

Siddons, Anne Rivers. *Peachtree Road.* New York: Harper & Row, Publishers, 1988.

Stevens, Preston Standish, FAIA. *Building a Firm, Stevens & Wilkinson, Inc.* Atlanta, 1980.

Timmis, Gail Morgan, ed. *Atlanta's Lasting Landmarks.* Atlanta Urban Design Commission, 1987.

Tipping, H. Avray. *English Homes, Early Georgian, 1714–1760.* London: Country Life, 1921.

White, Dana F. and Victor A. Kramer, eds. *Olmsted South.* Westport, Connecticut: Greenwood Press, 1979.

Williams, Eleanor. *Ivan Allen, "A Resourceful Citizen."* Atlanta: The Ivan Allen-Marshall

The Wren's Nest, Joel Chandler Harris's West End home, remodeled 1884.

Company, 1950.

Williford, William Bailey. *Peachtree Street, Atlanta.* Athens: University of Georgia Press, 1962.

Wilson, John Stainback. *Atlanta As It Is.* New York: Little, Rennie & Company, 1871.

Woodward, C. Vann. *Origins of the New South, 1877–1913.* Baton Rouge: Louisiana State University, 1951.

Wright, Ward H. *History of the Georgia Power Company.* Atlanta: The Georgia Power Company, 1957.

PERIODICALS

Askey, Linda C. "Dan's Garden." *Southern Living.* 22 (April 1987): 124–127.

Avery, Isaac W. "Atlanta, Its History and Advantages." In *City of Atlanta... the Gateway City of the South.* Louisville, Kentucky: The Inter-state Publishing Company, 1893.

Bates, Lincoln. "The Alonzo Herndon Home." *Southern Homes.* 3 (Spring 1985): 42, 44, 46.

Crook, Lewis Edmund, Jr. "Transience... or Tradition?" *Southern Architect and Building News.* 57 (April 1931): 15.

Cleghorn, Reese. "Young Man on the Go, Comer Jennings." *Atlanta.* 5 (October 1965): 78–82.

Ellis, William S. "Atlanta, Pacesetter City of the South." *National Geographic.* 135 (February 1969): 246–281.

Ennis, Michael. "Architects' Forum: Charles Moore." *Architectural Digest.* (September 1990): 72–78.

Grady, James. "A Question of Style, Houses in Atlanta, 1885–1900." *Yale Perspecta.* 15, 1975.

Galphin, Bruce. "Ho, Ho, Jova." *Atlanta.* 15 (December 1975): 35–36; 75-77; 120.

Galphin, Bruce and Steve Mayfield. "Ansley Park Fights Back." *Atlanta.* 4 (December 1964): 16–21.

Garrett, Franklin M. "Land Lots 105 and 106 of the 17th District of Fulton County, Georgia. Part I, Land Lot 106." *The Atlanta Historical Journal.* 27 (Spring 1983) 51–70.

——————. "Land Lots 105 and 106 of the 17th District of Fulton County, Georgia. Part II, Land Lot 105." *The Atlanta Historical Journal.* 27 (Summer 1983): 39–54.

Gill, Brendan. "The Malady of Gigantism." The *New Yorker.* (January 9, 1989): 73–77.

Griffin, Helen Candler, ed. "A Classic Cityscape Designed by Architect Neel Reid—the Tompkins House." *Southern Accents.* 9 (January-February 1986): 82–87.

Harte, Susan. "Urban Renewal in Midtown." *Atlanta Weekly, At Home.* (February 26, 1989): 18–21.

Haygood, Greene B. "Sketch of Atlanta." In William's *Atlanta Directory and City Guide.* Atlanta, 1859.

Helyar, John. "The Big Hustle." *The Wall Street Journal.* 211 (February 29, 1988): 1, 15.

Hooten, James A., ed. "Comer Jennings, Southern Artist." *Southern Accents.* 3 (Fall 1980): 82–85.

Maddox, Robert Foster. "Presidents Report." In *Atlanta Chambers of Commerce Annual Report.* (January 1906).

Martin, Jean. "Mule to Marta," Vol 1. 19 (November 2, 1975): 1–112.

Mitchell, William R., Jr. "The Architecture of James Means." *Southern Homes.* 7 (March/April 1989): 84–97.

——————. "The Swan House." *Southern Accents.* 8 (August 1985): 42–53.

Perkerson, Medora Field. "He [Neel Reid] Made Atlanta Beautiful." *The Atlanta Journal Magazine* (October 20, 1946): 6–7.

Reagan, Alice E. "Promoting the New South: Hannibal I. Kimball and Henry W. Grady." *The Atlanta Historical Journal.* 27 (Fall 1983): 5–19.

Reed, Henry Hope "America's Greatest Living Classical Architect, Philip Trammell Shutze of Atlanta, Georgia," *Classical America IV,* (1977): 5–46.

Sherrod, Robert. "Midtown." *Atlanta.* 13 (July 1973): 110–111; 148-154.

Shipp, Bill. "A Legend in Our Own Minds." *Atlanta.* 28 (January 1989): 39–41.

Shutze, Phil. "Problems of a Synagogue." *Southern Architectural Review.* 1 (September 1936): 10–15; 20.

Smith, Harvey, ed. "Design for a Residence for a Member of the Firm, Hentz, Adler, & Shutze." *Southern Architectural Review.* 2 (June 1937): 4–9.

Strong, Jack. "The Civil War Treasures of Beverly M. DuBose, Jr." *Southern Accents.* 1 (Winter 1978): 52–55.

Trillin, Calvin. "Atlanta: A City of Changing Slogans." *Time.* 132 (July 25, 1988): 30–32.

Zwingle, Erla. "Atlanta on the Rise." *National Geographic.* 174 (July 1988): 2–29.

A Century of Atlanta Architects
c. 1855–c. 1955

These architects, now retired or deceased, helped to build Atlanta in the century from the 1850s through the 1950s.

Adler, Rudolph S. (1889–1945), Hentz, Reid & Adler.

Bleckley, Haralson (1870–1933).

Bodin, Daniel H. (1895–1963), Frazier & Bodin.

Boutell, John (1814–1886).

Bond, George Harwell (1891–1952), Cooper, Bond & Cooper.

Brown, A. Ten Eyck (1878–1940).

Bruce, Alexander C. (1835–1927), Bruce & Morgan.

Bush-Brown, Harold (1889–1983), Bush-Brown, Gailey & Heffernan.

Chase, William J. J. (1884–1972).

Cooper, Joseph W., Jr. (1899–1974), and

Cooper, Samuel Inman (1894–1974), Cooper & Cooper.

Crook, Lewis Edmund, Jr., (1898–1967), Ivey & Crook.

Denny, Willis F. (1872–1905).

Dillon, John Robert (1872–1938), Morgan & Dillon.

Downing, Walter T. (1865–1918).

Dougherty, Edward (1876–1944).

Dozier, Henrietta Cuttino (1872–1947).

Edwards, William A. (1866–1939), Edwards & Sayward.

Ford, Clement Johnston (1906–retired).

Golucke, J. W. (1865–1907).

Hentz, Hal F. (1883–1972), Hentz, Reid & Adler.

Hopson, Charles H. (1856–1941).

Howell, Albert (1904–1974).

Ivey, Ernest Daniel (1887–1966), Ivey & Crook.

Lind, E. G. (1829–1909).

Marye, P. Thornton (1872–1935), Marye & Alger and Marye, Alger & Vinour.

Means, James (1904–1979).

Morgan, Thomas Henry (1857–1940), Bruce & Morgan and Morgan & Dillon.

Norrman, Gottfried L. (1846–1909).

Parkins, William H. (1836–1894).

Pauley, William C. (1893–1985), landscape architect.

Preacher, G. Lloyd (1882–1972).

Pringle, Robert S. (1883–1937), Pringle & Smith.

Reid, J. Neel (1885–1926), Hentz, Reid & Adler.

Robinson, Arthur Neal (1887–1958).

Sayward, William J. (1875–1945), Edwards & Sayward.

Shutze, Philip Trammell (1890–1982), Hentz, Shutze & Adler.

Smith, Francis Palmer (1886–1971), Pringle & Smith.

Stevens, Preston, Sr., (1896–1989), Stevens & Wilkinson

Stewart, George W. (1862–1937).

Stoddart, W. L. (1896–1940).

Toombs, Henry Johnston (1896–1967), Toombs & Creighton.

Tucker, McKendree A., Sr., (1896–1972), Tucker & Howell.

Wachendorff, Eugene C. (1880–1957).

Wheeler, Lorenzo B. (1854–1899), Wheeler & Downing.

Wilburn, Leila Ross (1885–1967).

Above: Administration Building at the Georgia Institute of Technology, 1885; the school of architecture opened in 1908.

222

INDEX OF HOUSES IN
LANDMARK HOMES OF ATLANTA

The Tullie Smith house, c. 1845, was moved from Dekalb County to the grounds of the Atlanta Historical Society and is open to the public as a museum of antebellum life in the Atlanta area.

Beath-Griggs House	66	Jennings House	186
Black House	168	Martin Luther King Birth Home	78
Blount House	74	Lanier Apartment	102
Calhoun-Thornwell House	116	Lullwater House	92
Callanwolde	88	Martin House	157
Clark Atlanta University President's Home	83	Nicolson-McCord House	72
DuBose House	200	Nixon-Watson House	122
Efird House	164	Orme-Davison-Block House	160
Franklin Cottage	196	Parker-Hale House	108
Glenn House, Glenridge Hall	94	Patterson-Carr House	153
Goodrum-Abreu-Rushton House	138	Ray House, "The Barclay"	194
Governor's Mansion	144	Reynolds Cottage, Spelman College	82
Grant-Jones House	106	Rhodes Hall	98
Griffin House	204	Richardson-Franklin House	148
Hentz-Lane-Morrison House	190	Rooker Penthouse	214
Herndon House	84	Smith House, Bellmere	208
Howell House	180	Swan House	129
Howell-McDowell House	175	Tompkins House	110
Inman House	210	Thornton-Jones House	142

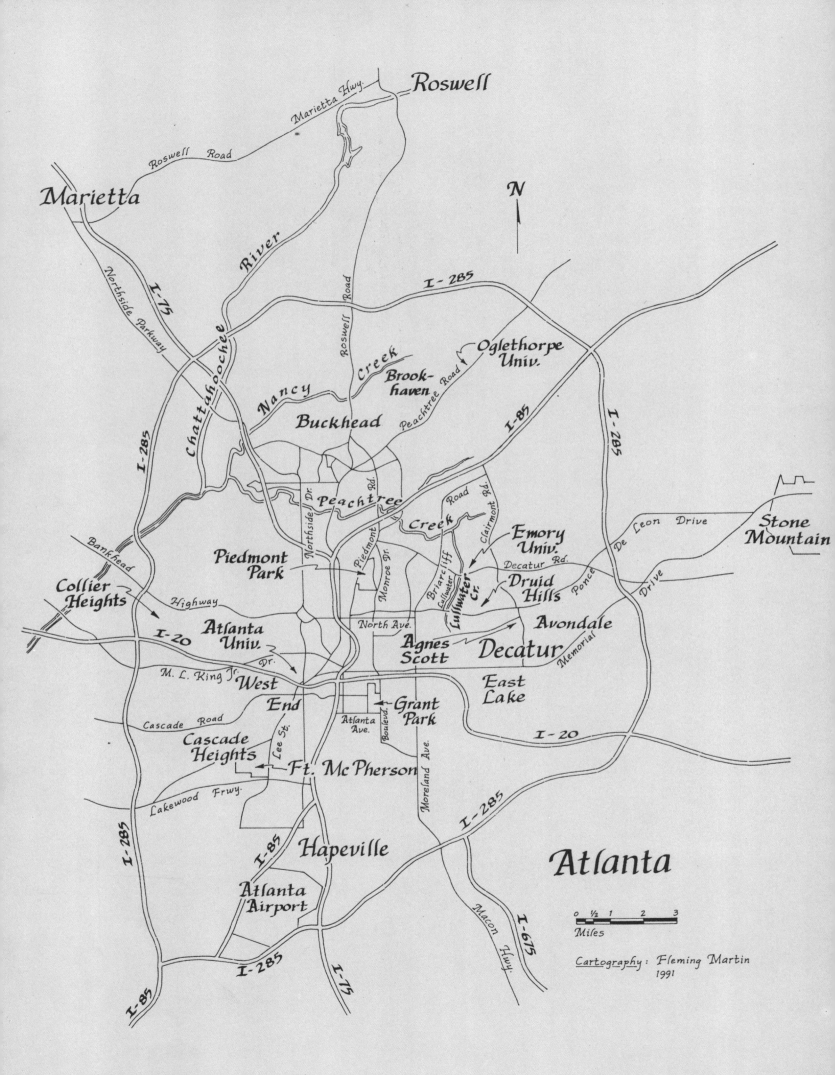

Roswell

Marietta

Marietta Hwy.

Roswell Road

Northside Parkway

I-75

N

Chattahoochee River

Nancy

Creek

Roswell Road

I-285

Brook-
haven

Oglethorpe
Univ.

Peachtree Road

Buckhead

I-85

I-285

Northside Dr.

Piedmont Rd.

Peachtree

Creek

Road

Clairmont Rd.

De Leon Drive

Stone
Mountain

I-285

Bankhead

Piedmont
Park

Piedmont

Monroe Dr.

Briarcliff

Lullwater

Emory
Univ.

Decatur Rd.

Ponce

Drive

Collier
Heights

Highway

Atlanta
Univ.

Lullwater Cr.

Druid
Hills

North Ave.

Avondale

I-20

Dr.

Agnes
Scott

Decatur

Memorial

M. L. King Jr.

West

East
Lake

Cascade Road

End

Lee St.

Atlanta
Ave.

Bouleva.

Grant
Park

Moreland Ave.

I-20

Cascade
Heights

Ft. McPherson

Lakewood Frwy.

I-285

I-85

Hapeville

Atlanta

Macon Hwy.

I-675

Atlanta
Airport

I-285

I-75

0 ½ 1 2 3
Miles

Cartography: Fleming Martin
1991